20 WAYS TO DRAW A CAT

AND 44 OTHER AWESOME ANIMALS

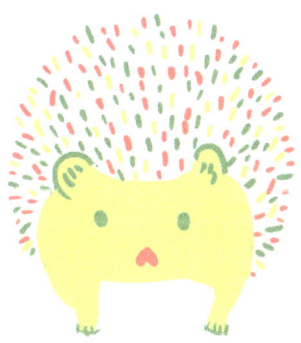

JULIA KUO

A Sketchbook for Artists, Designers, and Doodlers

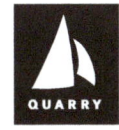

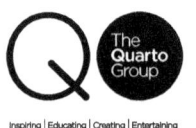

Brimming with creative inspiration, how-to projects, and useful information to enrich your everyday life, quarto.com is a favorite destination for those pursuing their interests and passions.

© 2013 by Quarry Books

Illustrations © 2013 Julia Kuo
Text © 2013 Julia Kuo

First published in 2013 by Quarry Books,
an imprint of The Quarto Group,
100 Cummings Center, Suite 265-D,
Beverly, MA 01915, USA.
T (978) 282-9590 F (978) 283-2742
Quarto.com

All rights reserved. No part of this book may be reproduced in any form without written permission of the copyright owners. All images in this book have been reproduced with the knowledge and prior consent of the artists concerned, and no responsibility is accepted by producer, publisher, or printer for any infringement of copyright or otherwise, arising from the contents of this publication. Every effort has been made to ensure that credits accurately comply with information supplied. We apologize for any inaccuracies that may have occurred and will resolve inaccurate or missing information in a subsequent reprinting of the book.

Quarry Books titles are also available at discount for retail, wholesale, promotional, and bulk purchase. For details, contact the Special Sales Manager by email at specialsales@quarto.com or by mail at The Quarto Group, Attn: Special Sales Manager, 100 Cummings Center, Suite 265-D, Beverly, MA 01915, USA.

ISBN: 978-1-59253-838-6

Digital edition published in 2013
eISBN: 978-1-61058-764-8

Library of Congress Control Number 2012953756

Design: Debbie Berne

CONTENTS

	Introduction 4	
Draw 20 ...	Cats 6	Kangaroos 52
	Tropical Birds 8	Lizards 54
	Giraffes 10	Zebras 56
	Elephants 12	Llamas & Alpacas 58
	Songbirds 14	Buffaloes 60
	Bugs 16	Mice 62
	Bears 18	Monkeys & Apes 64
	Fish 20	Otters 66
	Deer 22	Birds of Prey 68
	Octopi 24	Ostriches 70
	Dogs 26	Skunks 72
	Rabbits 28	Whales 74
	Sheep 30	Walruses 76
	Squirrels 32	Horses 78
	Lions 34	Hippopotamuses 80
	Turtles 36	Flamingos 82
	Tigers 38	Pigs 84
	Rhinoceroses 40	Penguins & Puffins 86
	Frogs 42	Sharks 88
	Raccoons 44	Camels 90
	Foxes 46	Sea Lions 92
	Hedgehogs 48	Snails 94
	Jellyfish 50	
		About the Artist 96

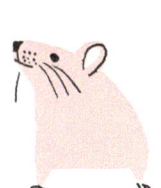

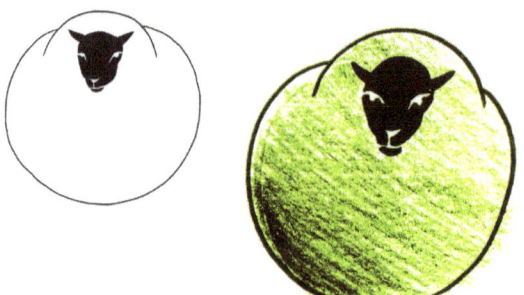

INTRODUCTION

Let's learn how to draw animals together! There are few things more fascinating and beautiful on Earth than animals. They come in all shapes and forms—from tiny birds to gigantic elephants, sweet deer to sly foxes, and striped zebras to spotted giraffes. You can pick your favorite animals from this book to draw, or you can think of animals that I haven't included. There are forty-five different types of animals in this book, but that's just a tiny number out of all the animals out there! Next time you are at the zoo, keep an eye out for the unusual animals you haven't heard of before. For example, have you ever heard of a *capybara*? A capybara is the largest rodent in the world. That means it belongs to the same family as squirrels and bunnies, but it is as big as a dog!

Even the same types of animals come in so many varieties that it's impossible to draw them just one way. At first glance, a family of zebras might look very similar, but if you look closely you will notice that they don't have the same identical stripes. Think of yourself—you might look a little bit like the rest of your family, but you don't look exactly like them. Every single animal looks special in its own way, so I made sure that each drawing is a little different from the last.

HOW TO USE THIS BOOK

These drawings are all made up of a combination of lines, shapes, and patterns. Look for squares, circles, straight lines, and squiggly lines to help break down the pictures, and then try copying the different animal drawings using those simple elements. Draw the big shapes and lines first, and then add in the smaller details.

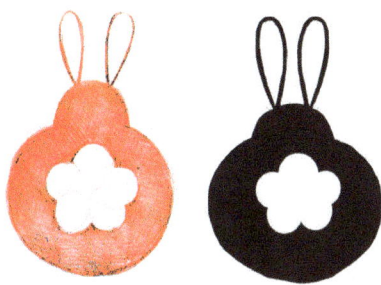

If you have tracing paper, you can trace the drawings directly, but don't worry about getting them exactly the same. When you think you have gotten the hang of it, try drawing your own!

Try to start out with a pencil and eraser so that you're not afraid of making mistakes. When you feel more comfortable with drawing, explore by using many different types of tools—pens, colored pencils, markers, or even paints. Color in the existing drawings and then color in your own drawings. If you are feeling especially adventurous, you can cut out paper shapes and paste them on the blank pages. It's always fun to try as many things as possible to decide what you like the best.

See how many different pictures you can come up with of your favorite animals. How many ways can you draw a turtle shell? You can make it a circle, square, or irregular shape. Think about what you can draw inside the shell. You can fill it with stripes, little spots, big spots, squares of different sizes, or just fill it in with a solid color. You can also decide to draw nothing inside the shell if you think it looks best that way, since sometimes less is more.

Don't forget to show your friends and family when you're done. Or even better yet, ask them if they want to make some drawings of their favorite animals, too!

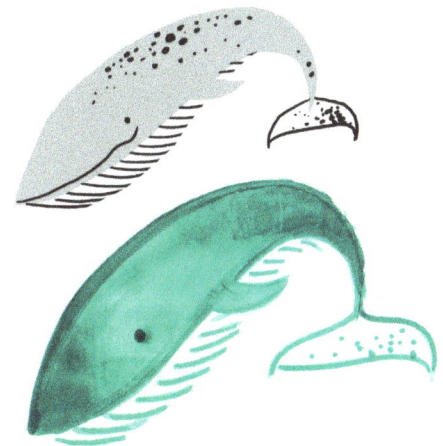

sheep: marker and colored pencil
songbirds: marker and watercolor
rabbits: colored pencil
whales: watercolor

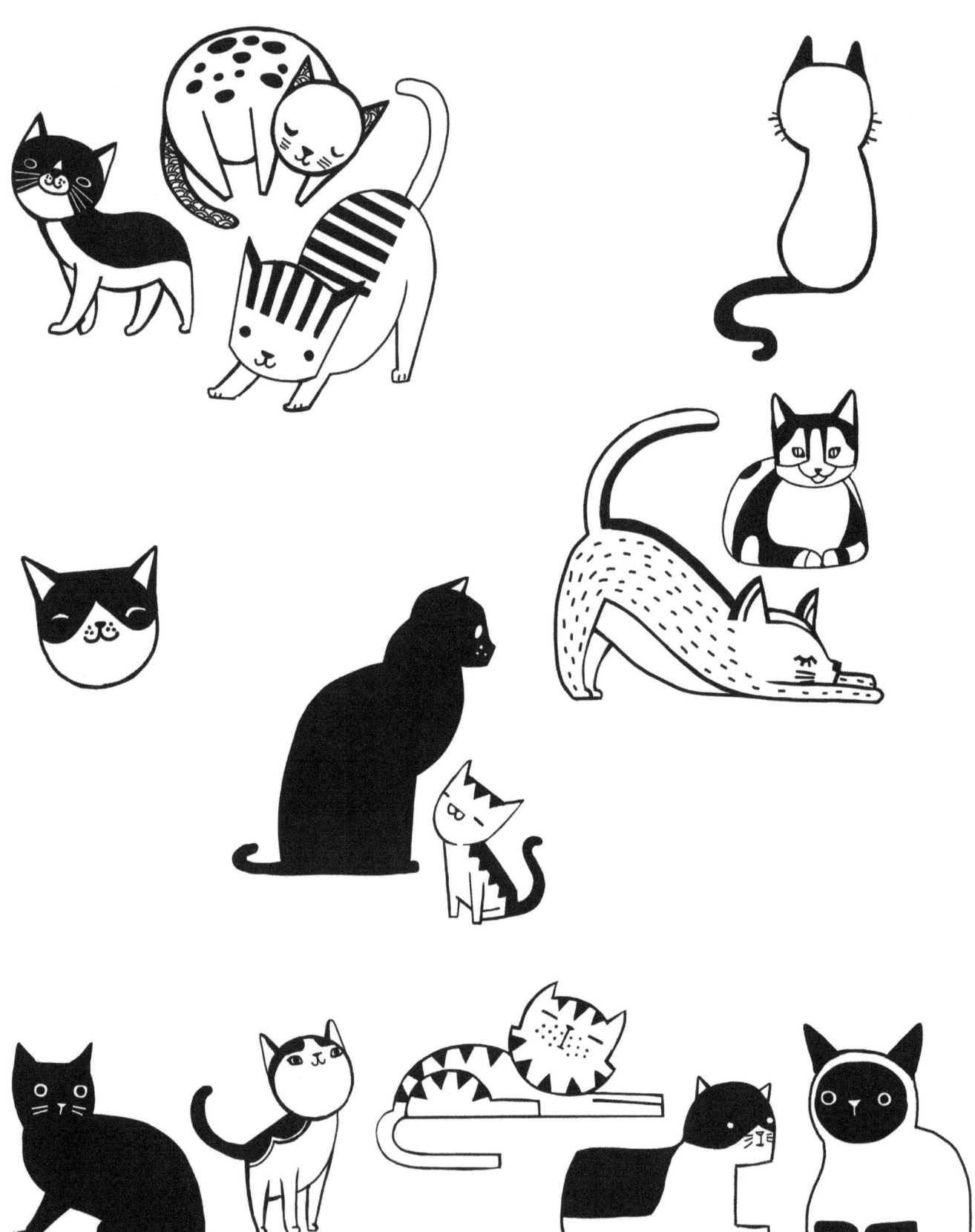

DRAW 20
cats

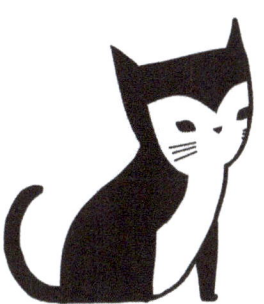
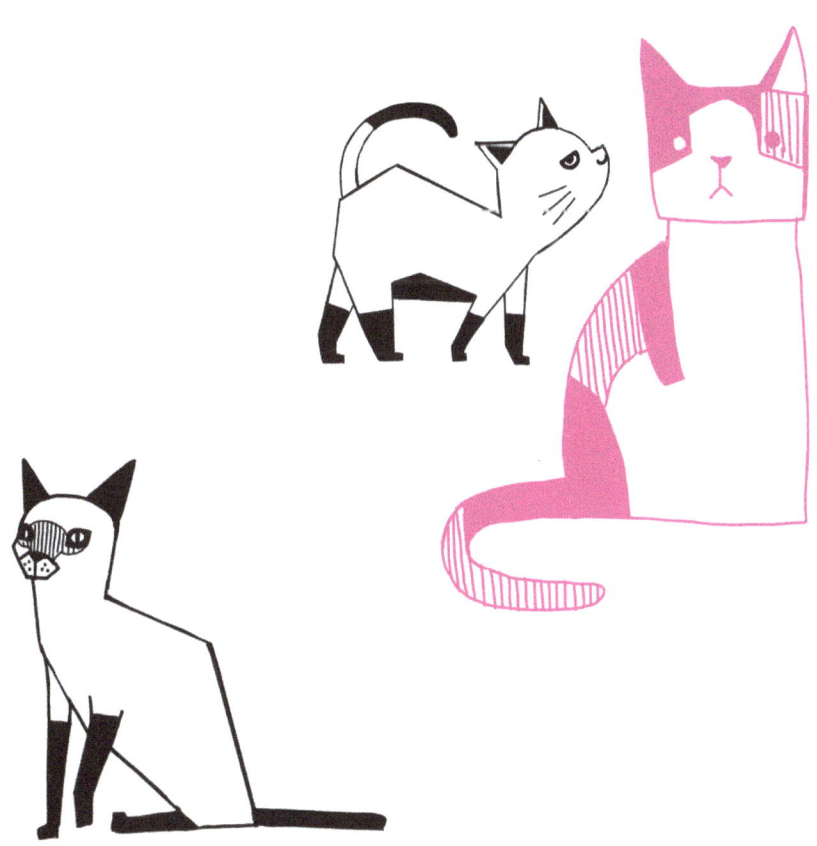
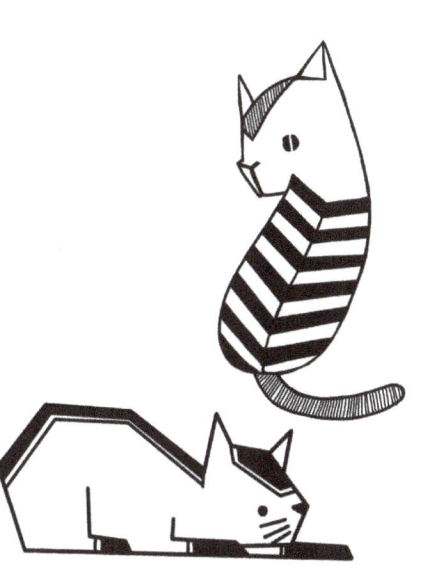

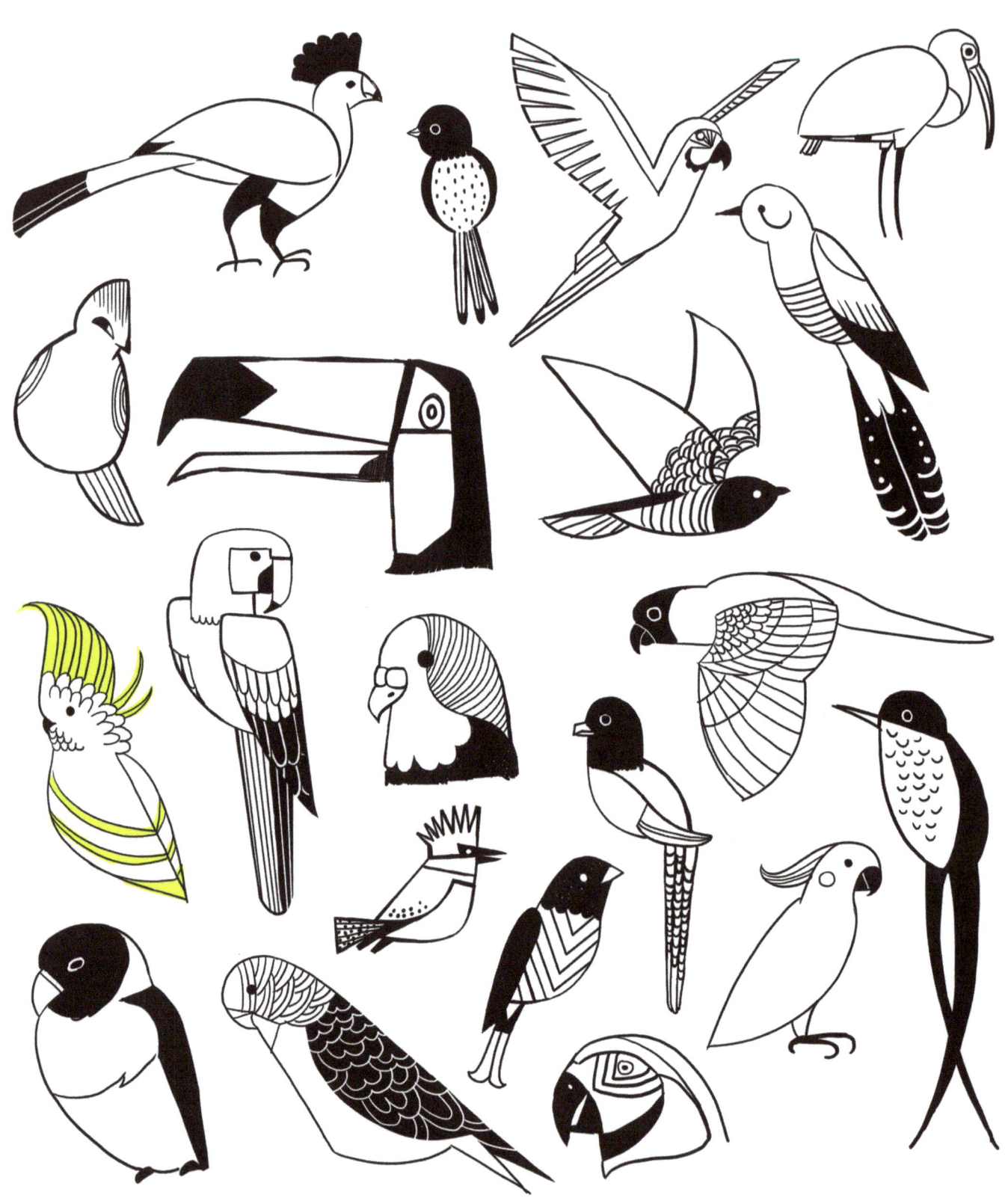

DRAW 20 TROPICAL BIRDS

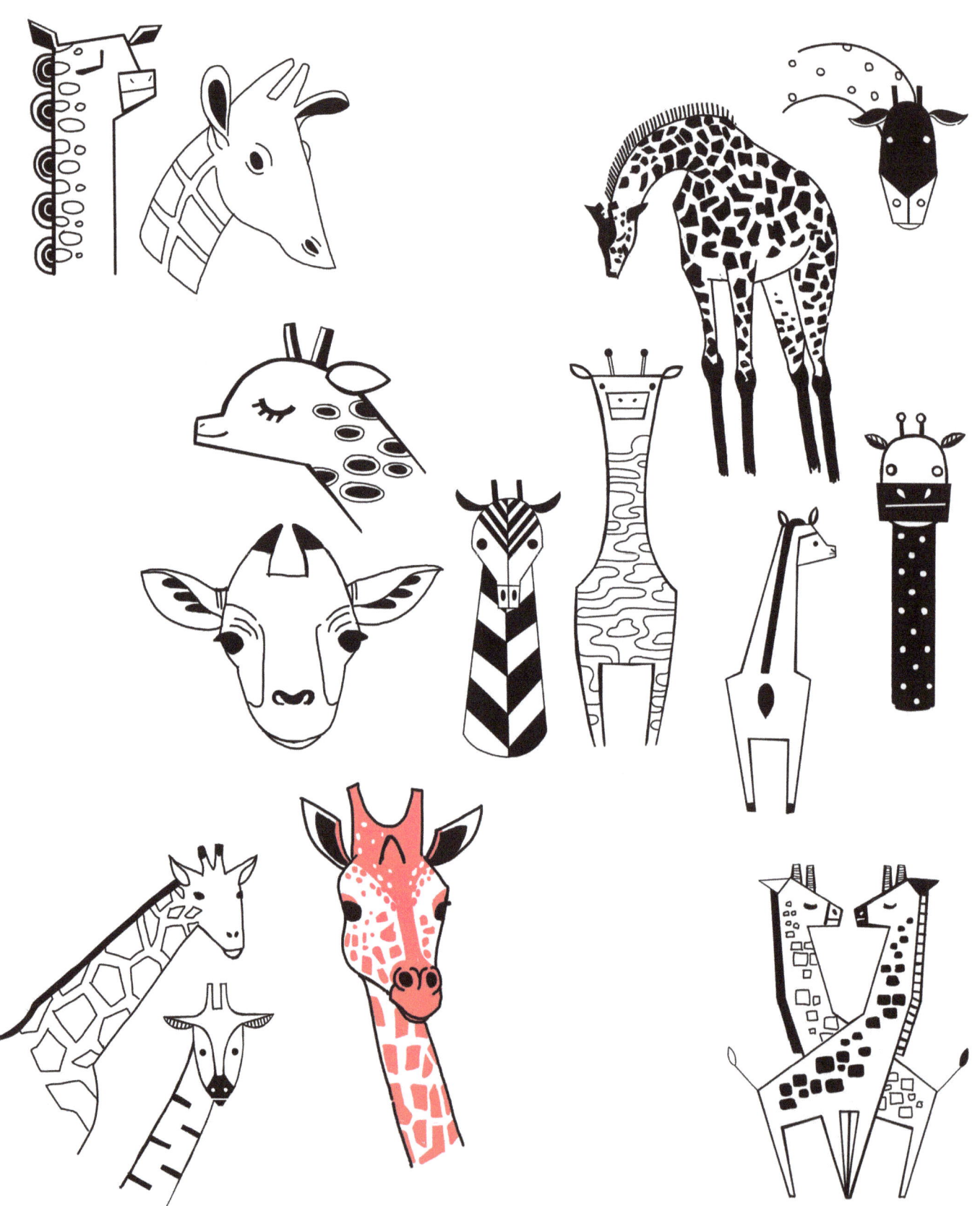

DRAW 20
Giraffes

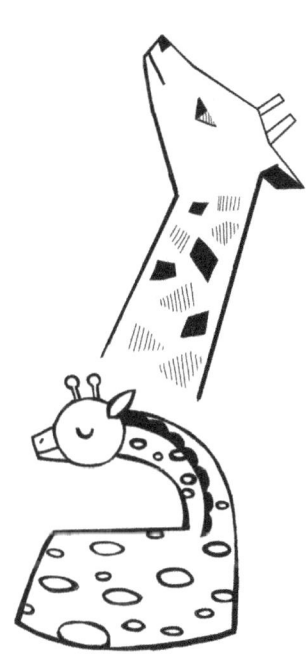

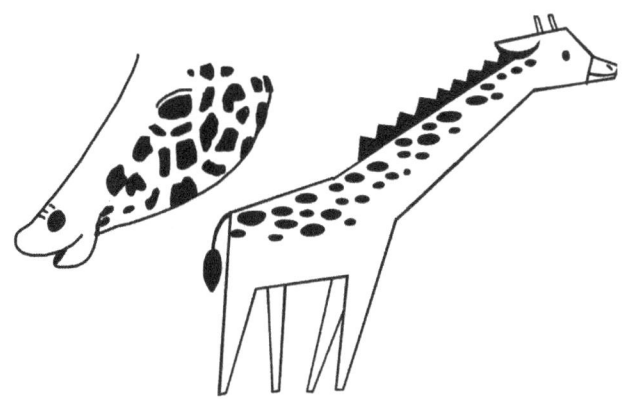

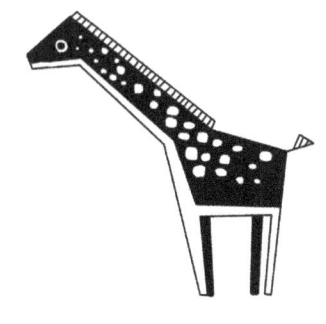

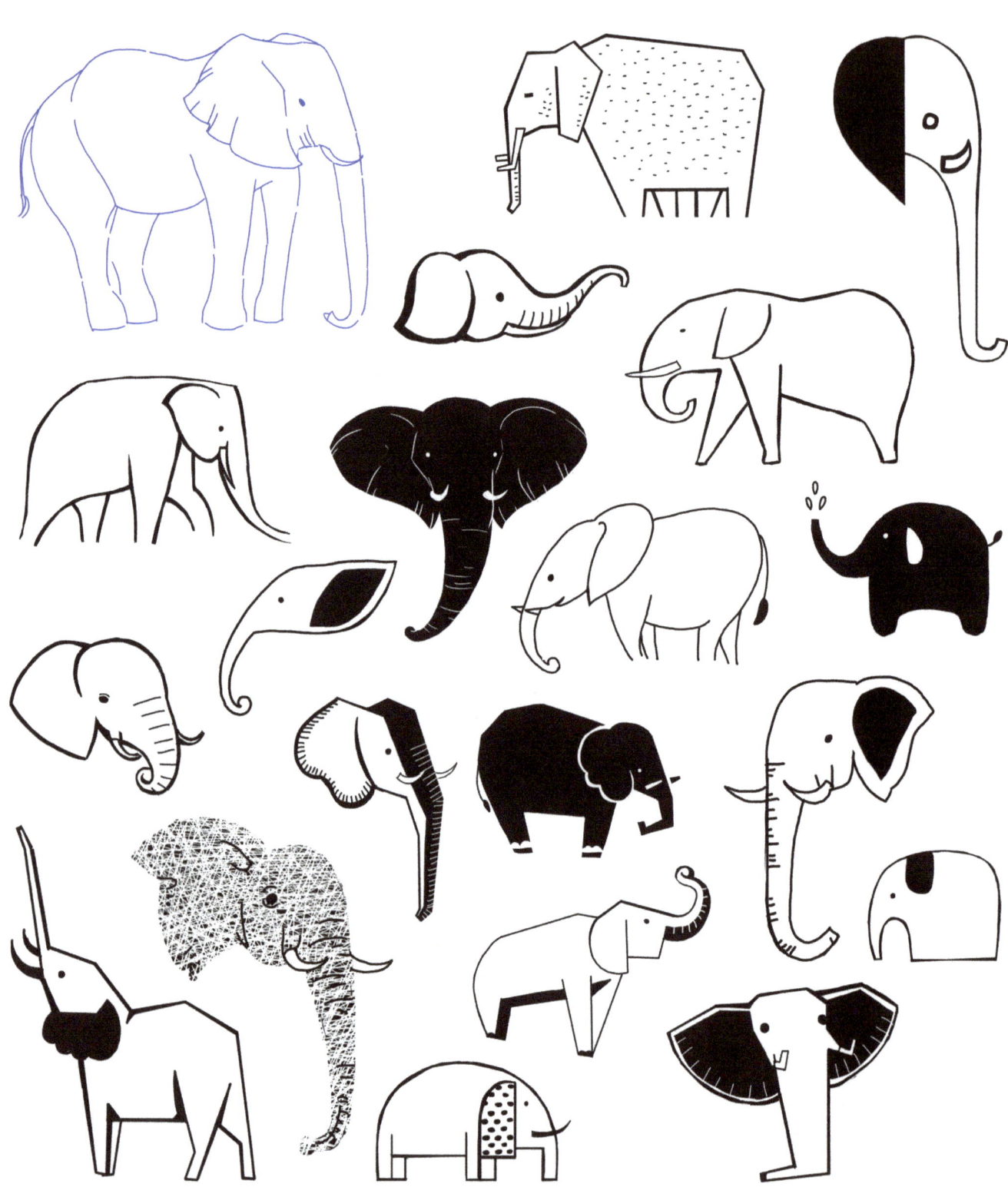

DRAW 20 elephants

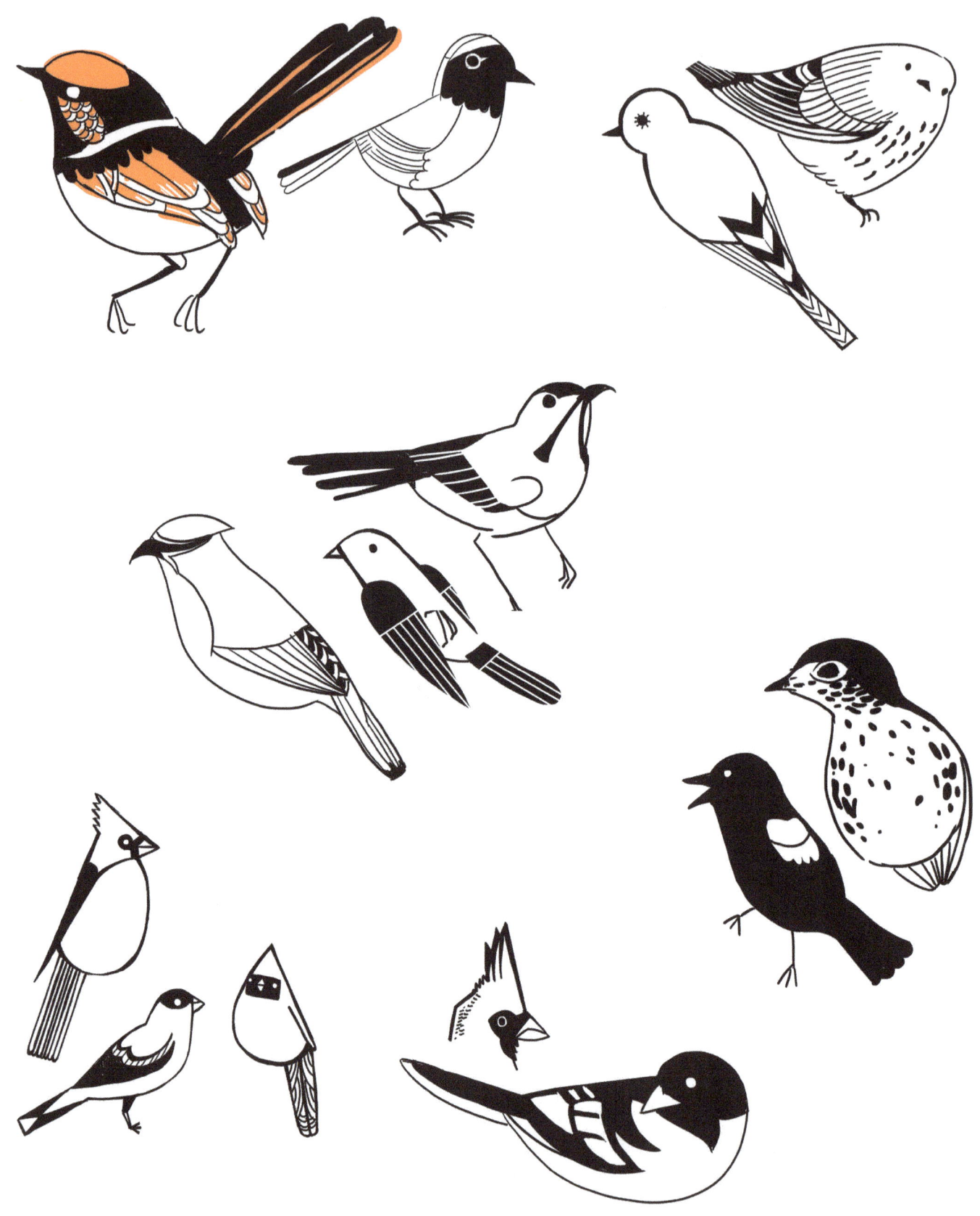

DRAW 20 Songbirds

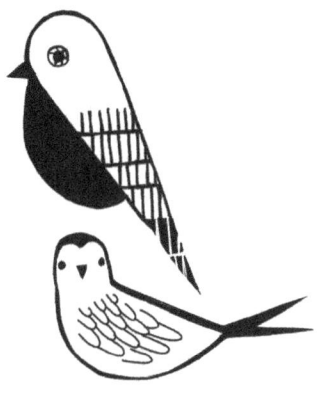
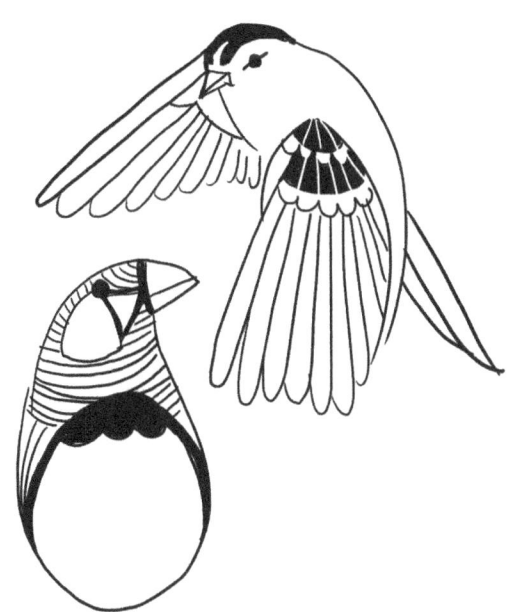
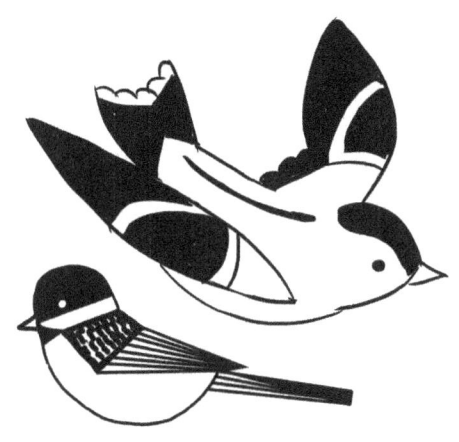

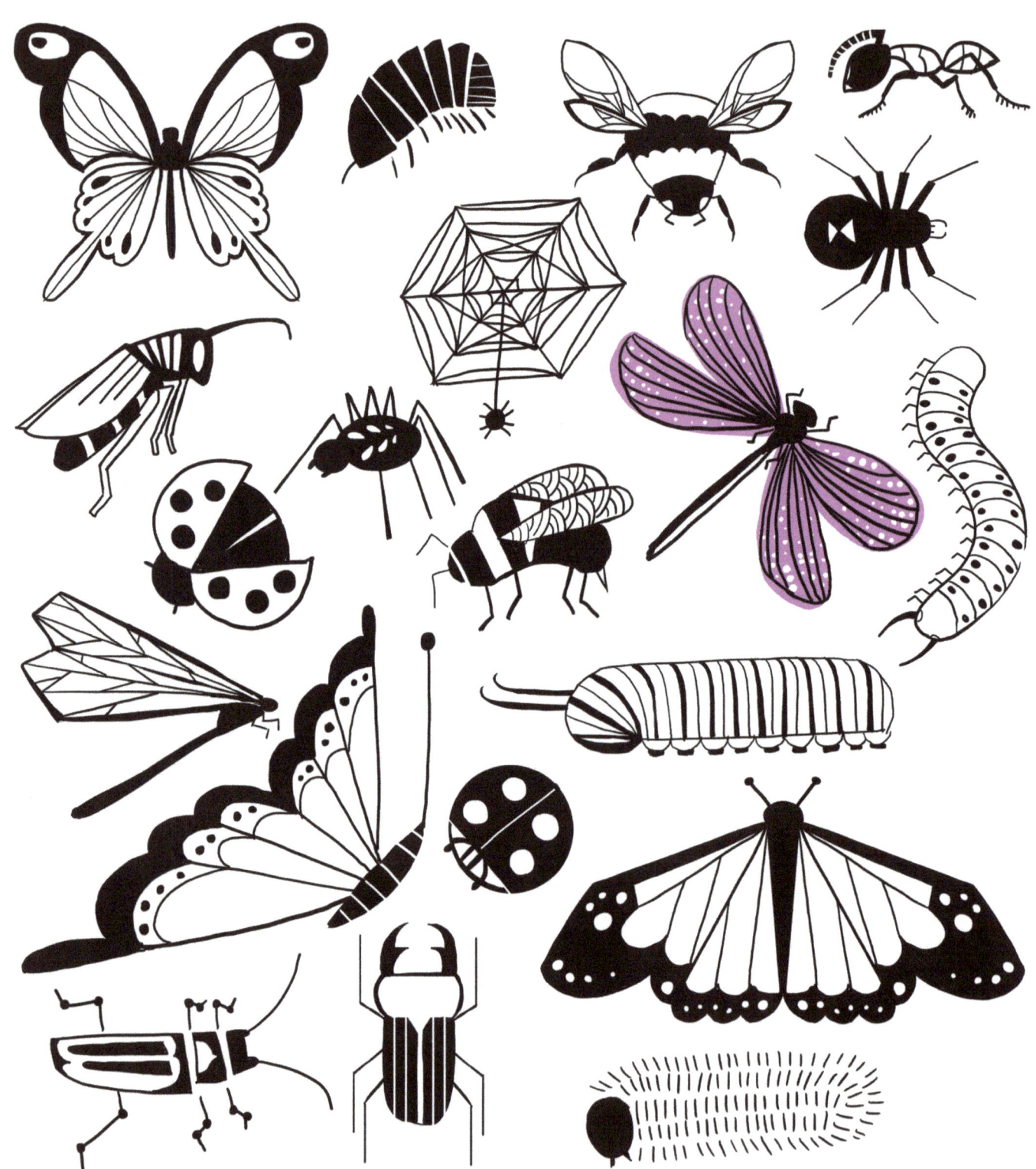

DRAW 20
BUGS

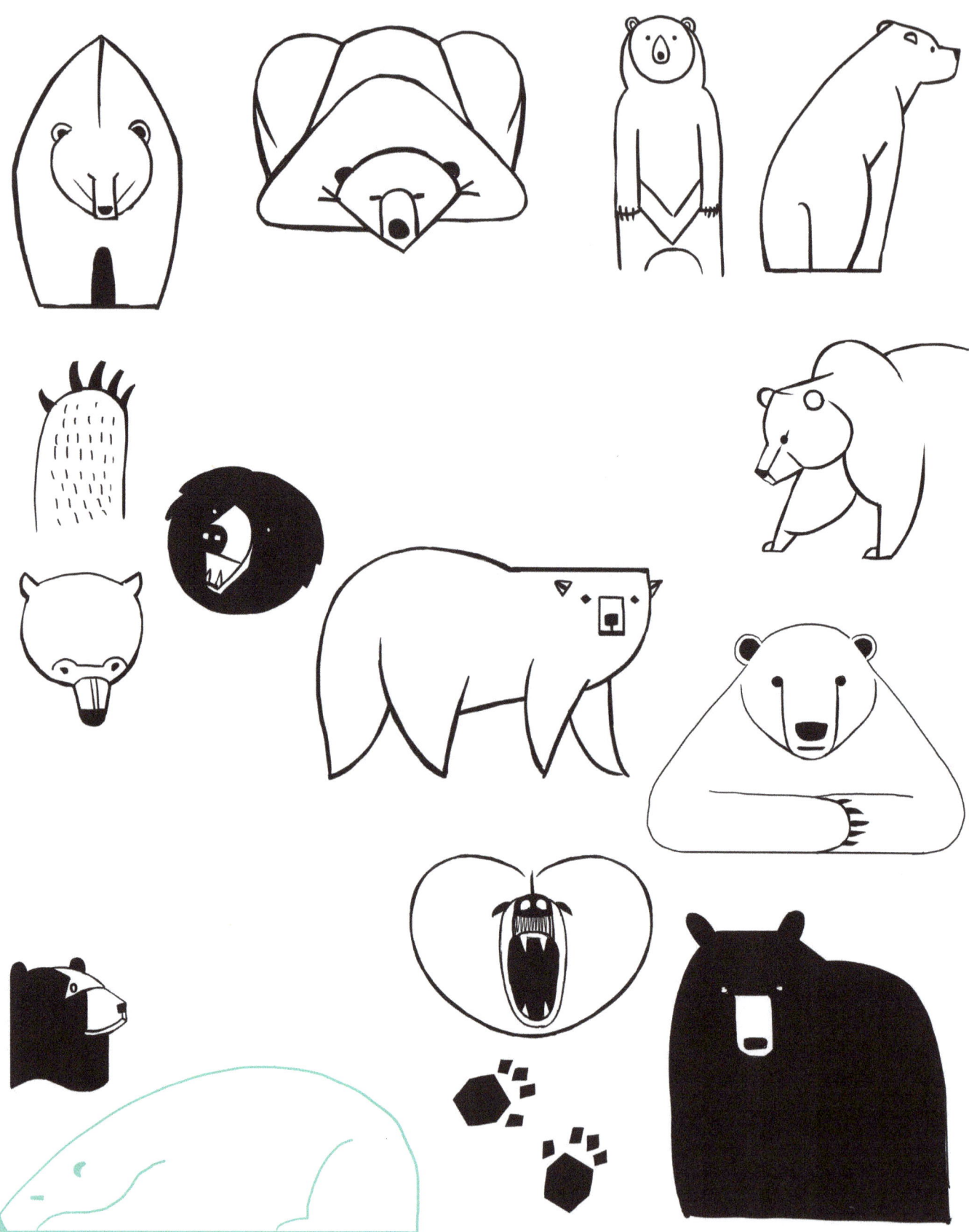

DRAW 20
BEARS

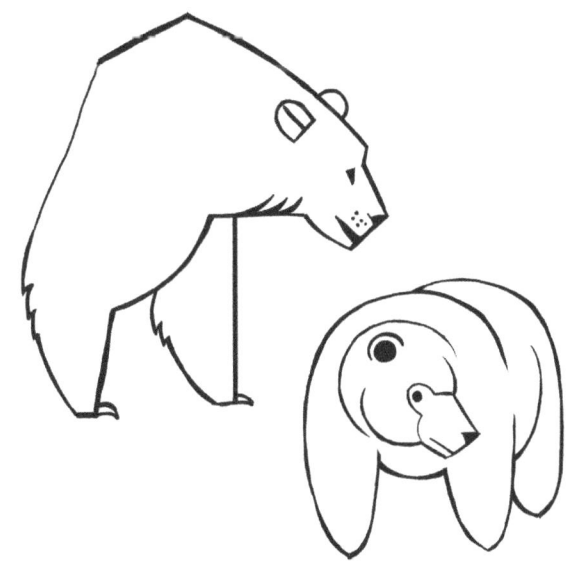
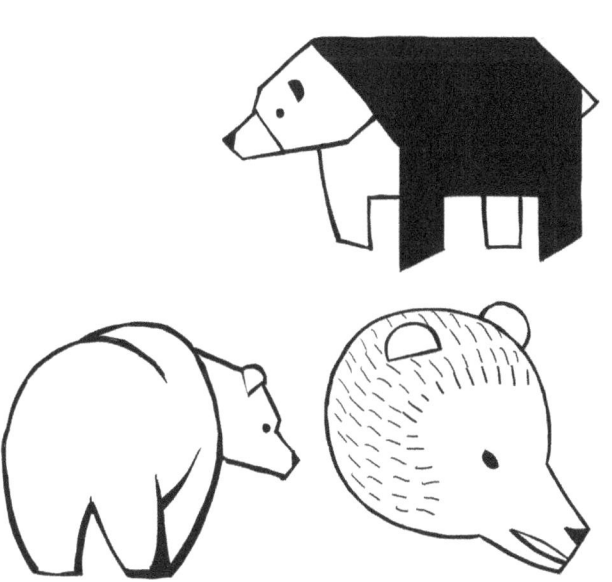

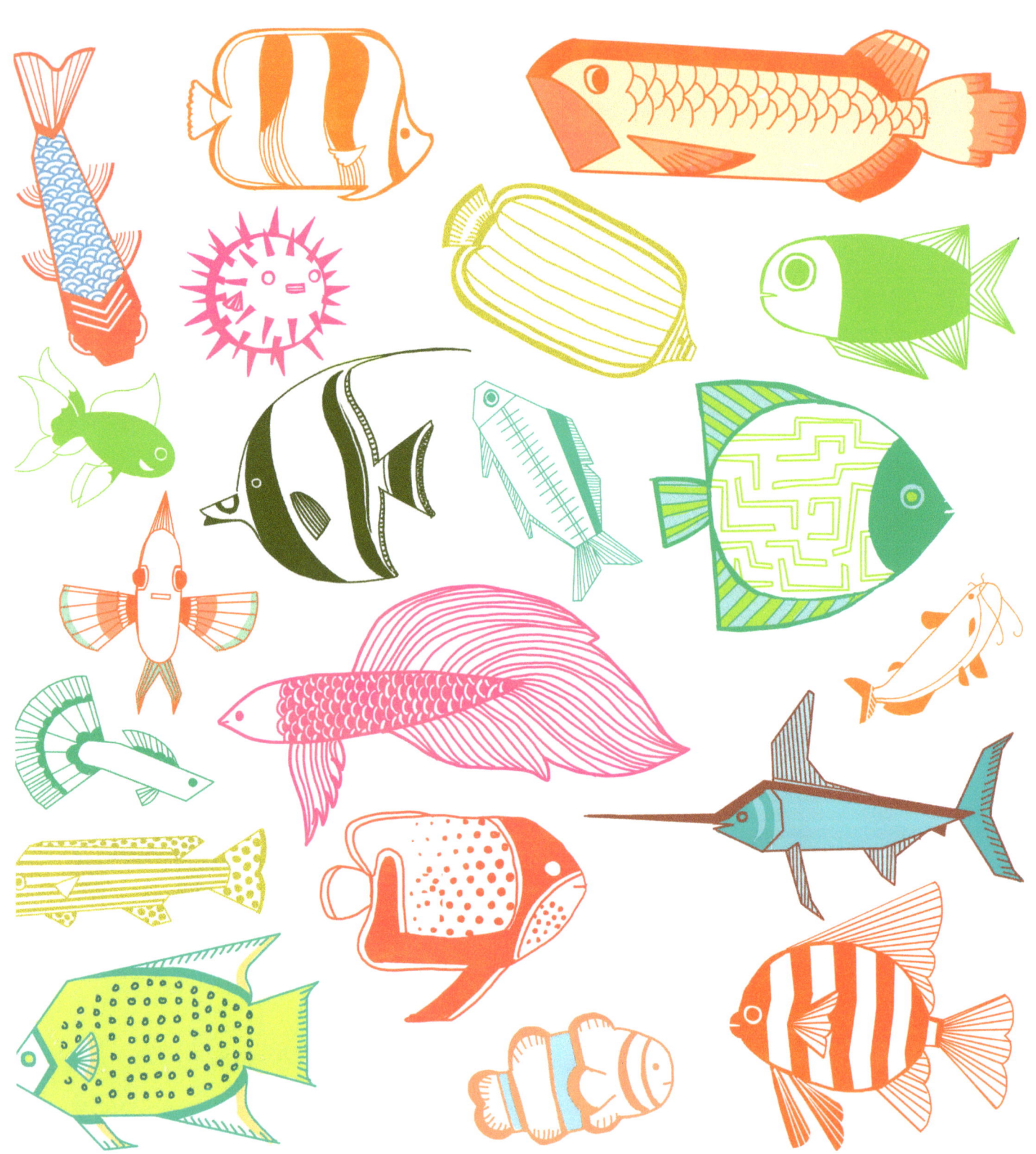

DRAW 20 fish

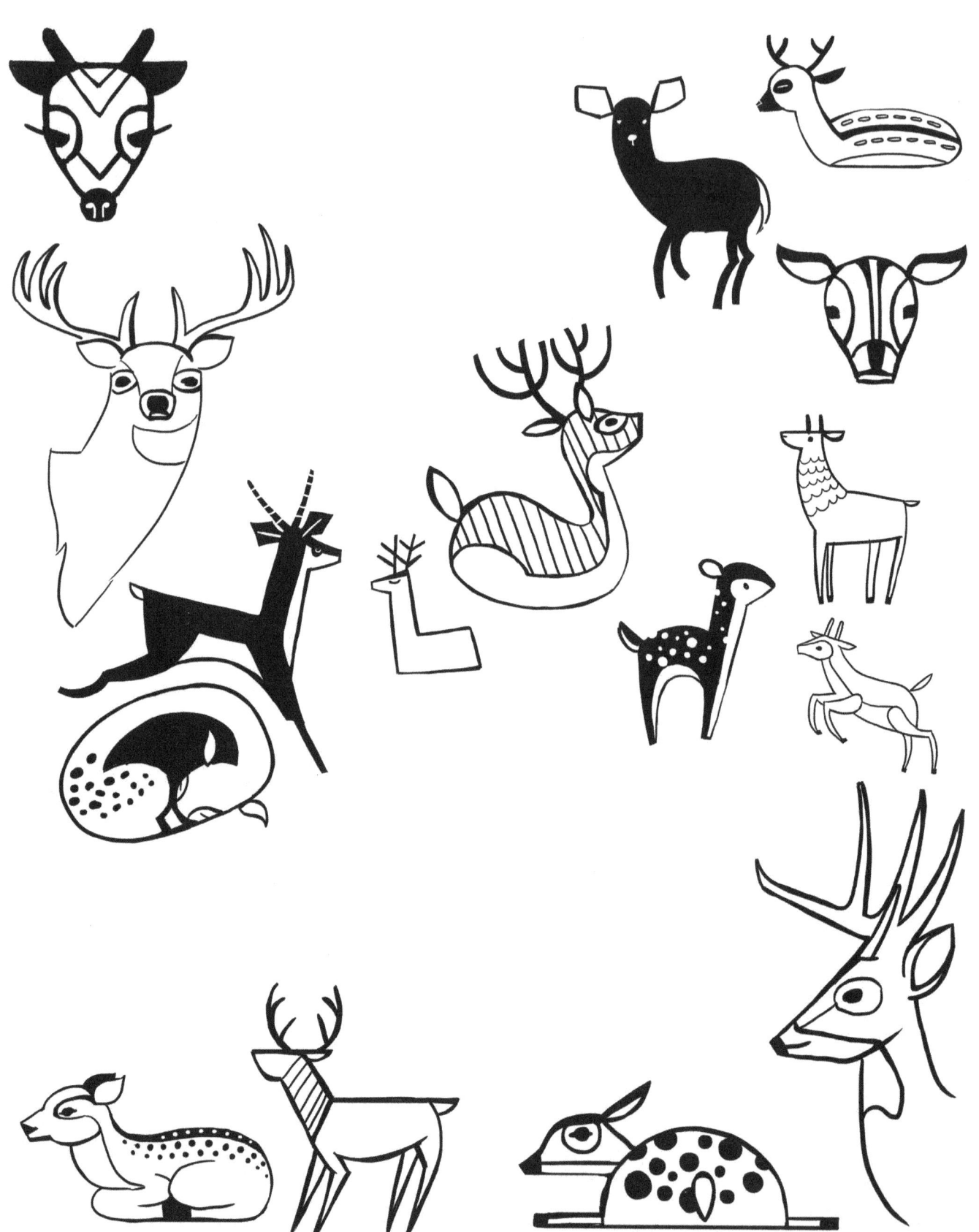

DRAW 20
DEER

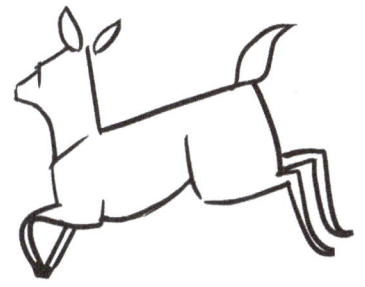

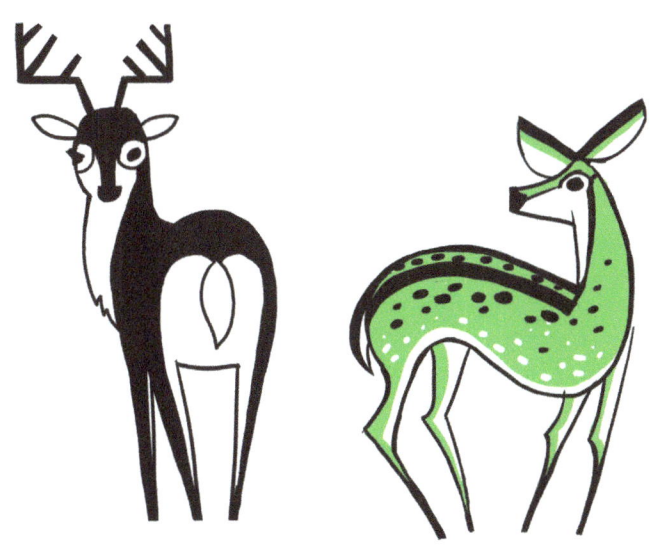

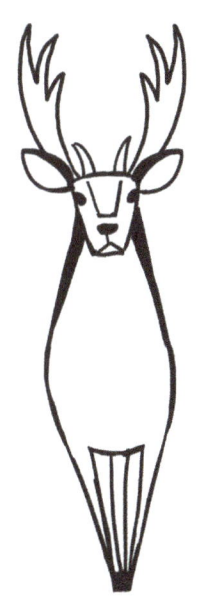

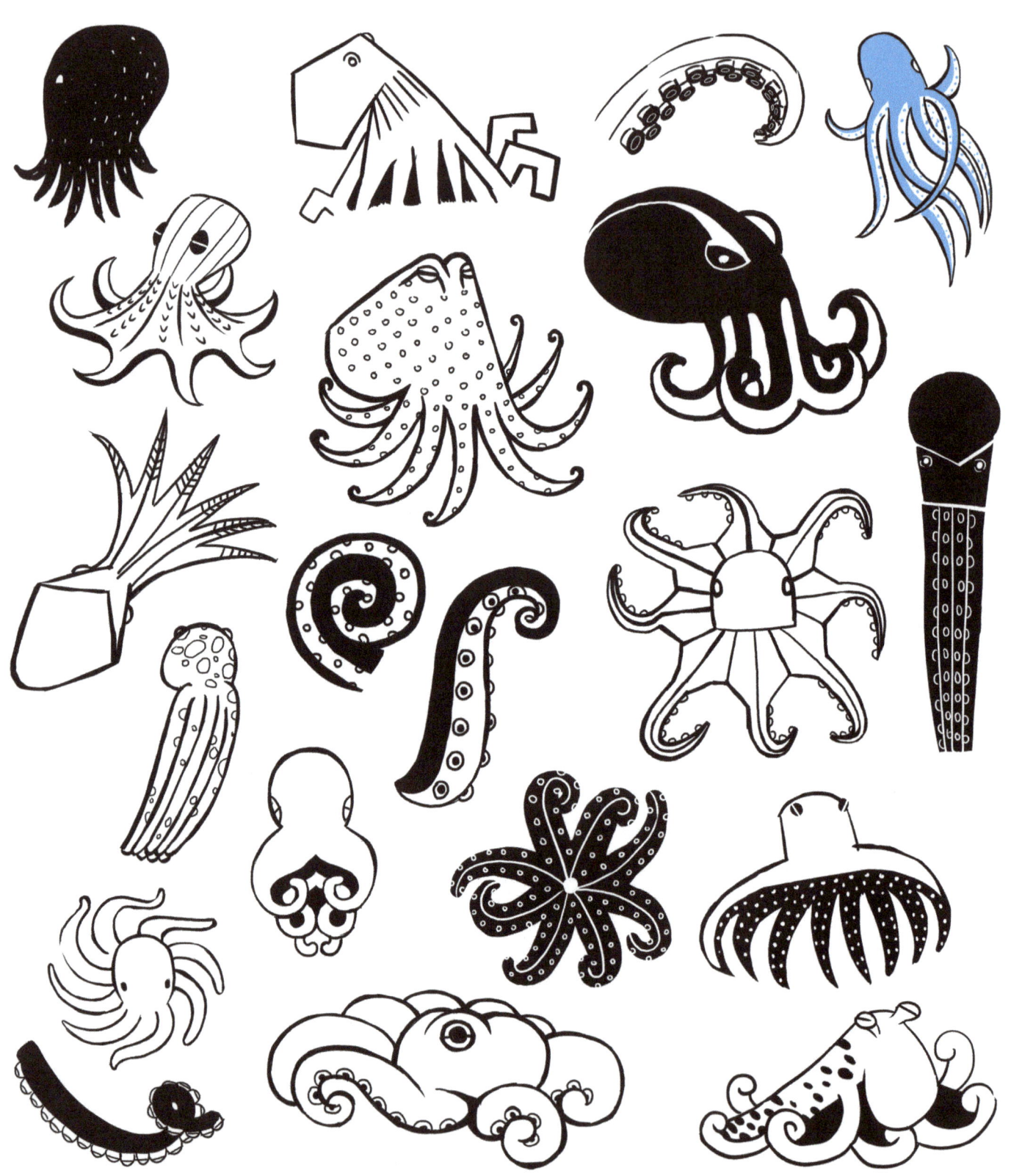

DRAW 20 octopi

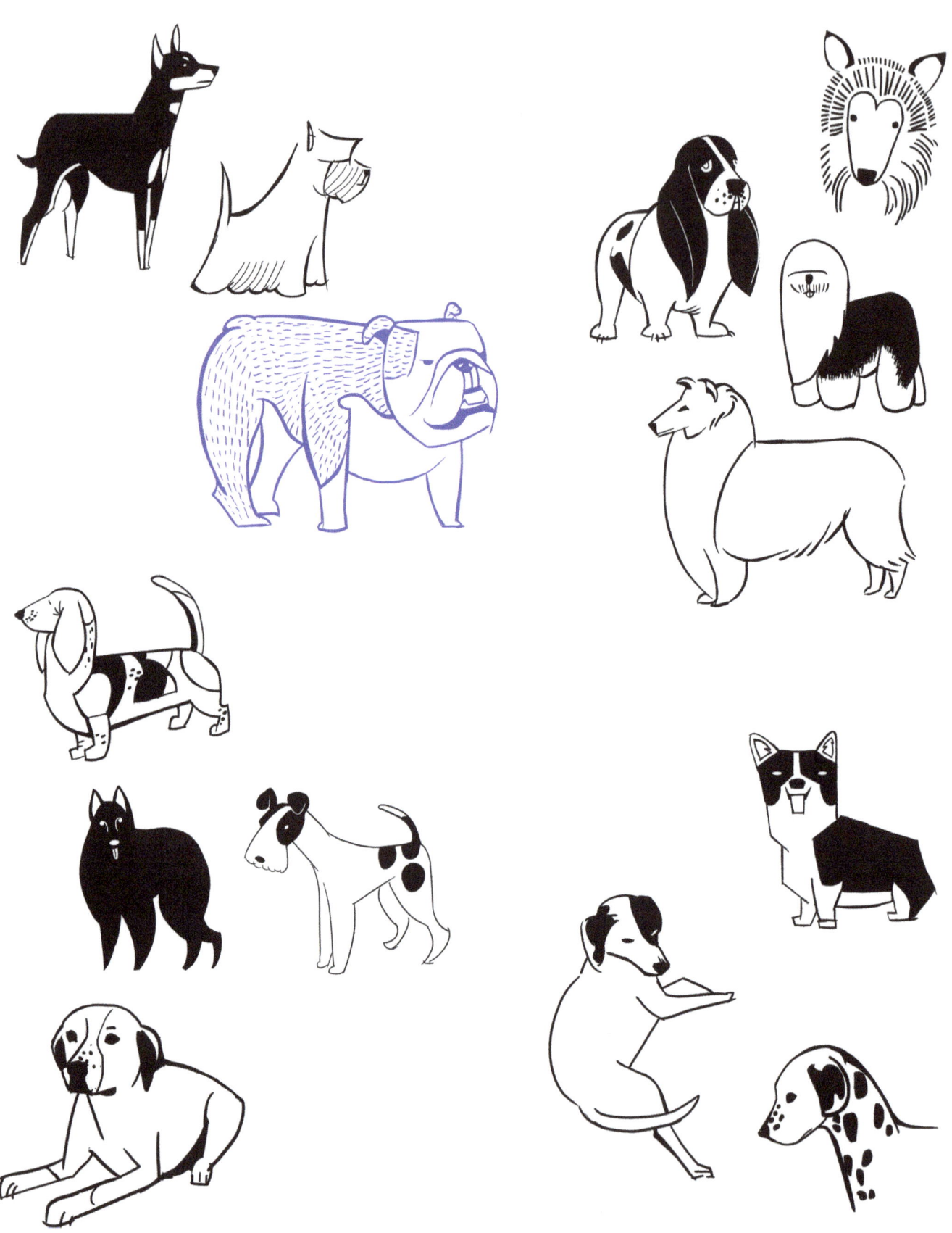

DRAW 20
DOGS

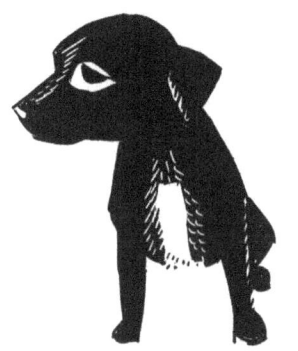
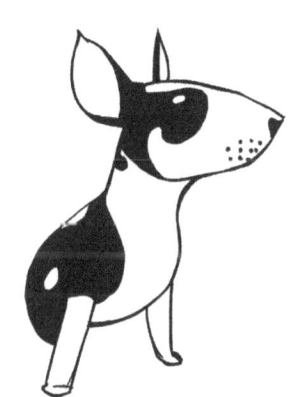
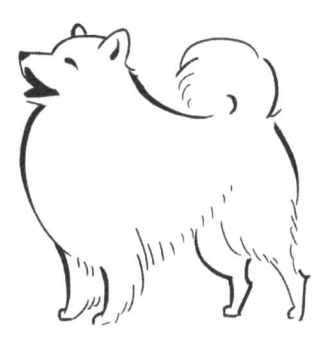
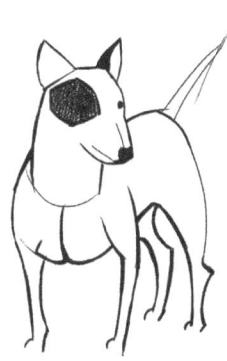
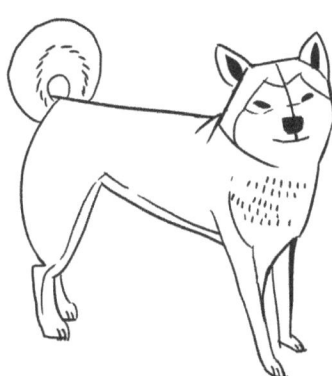
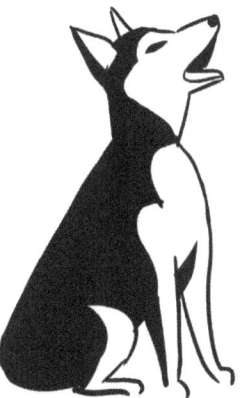

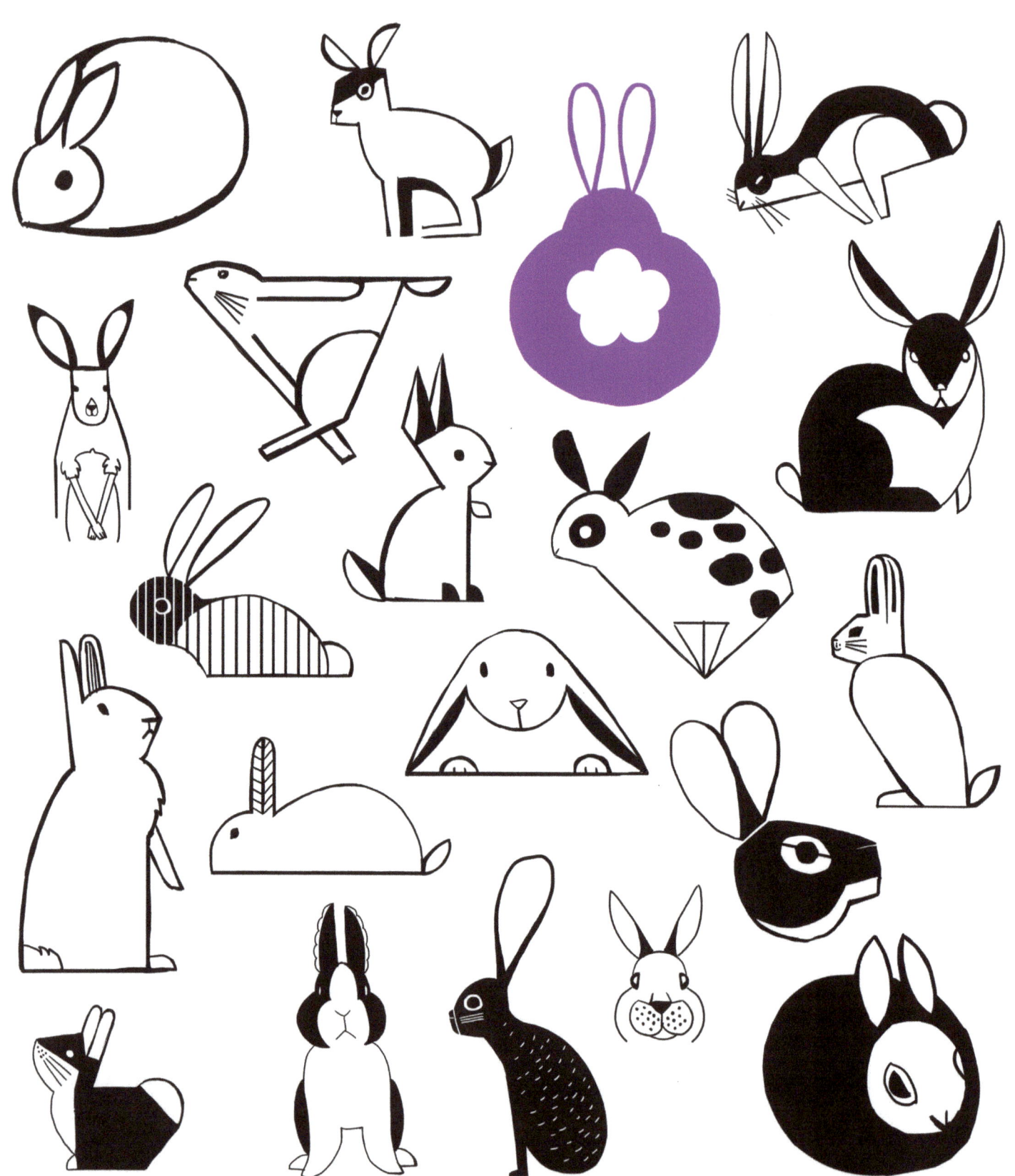

DRAW 20
rabbits

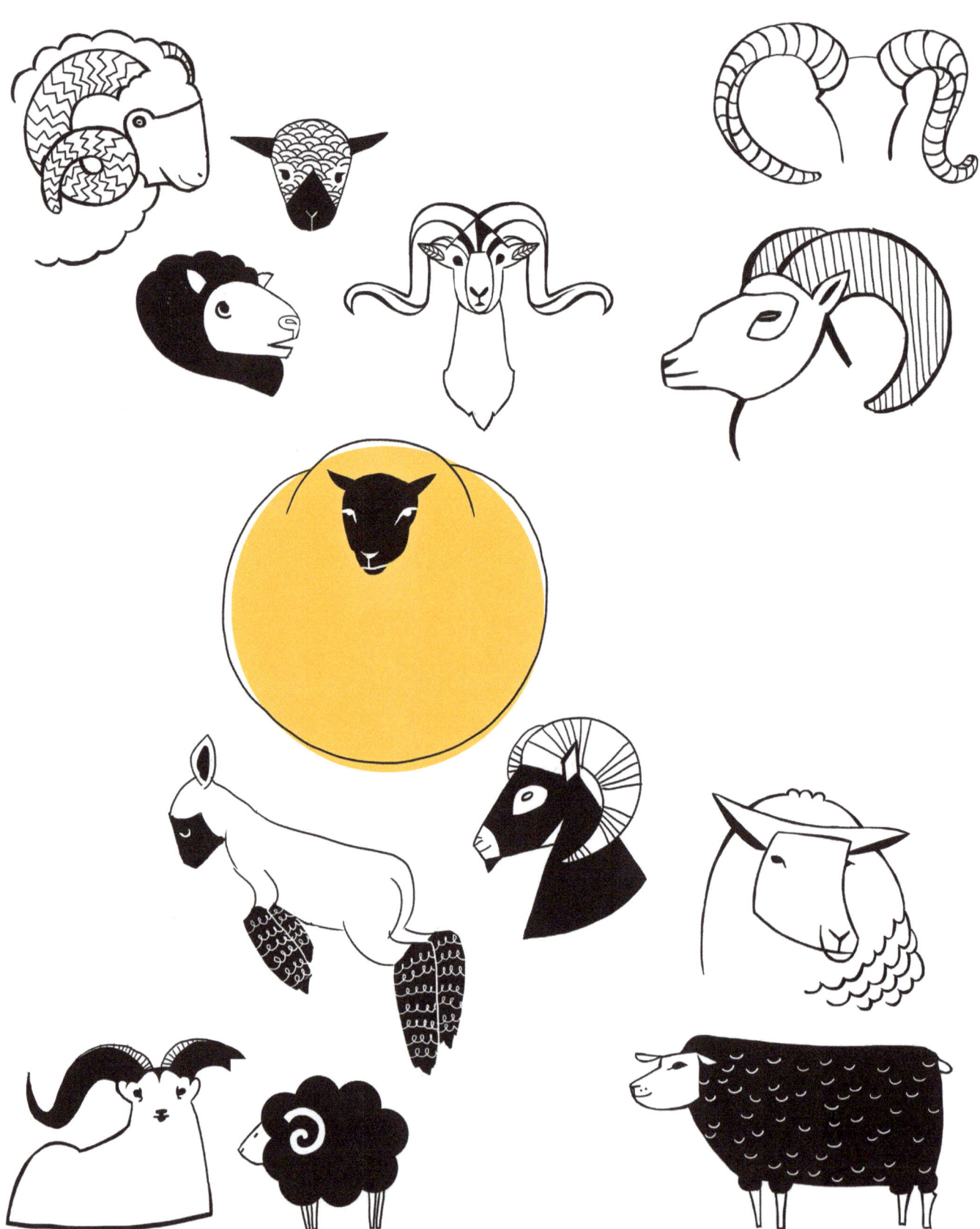

DRAW 20
sheep

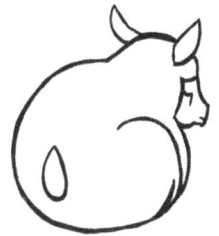

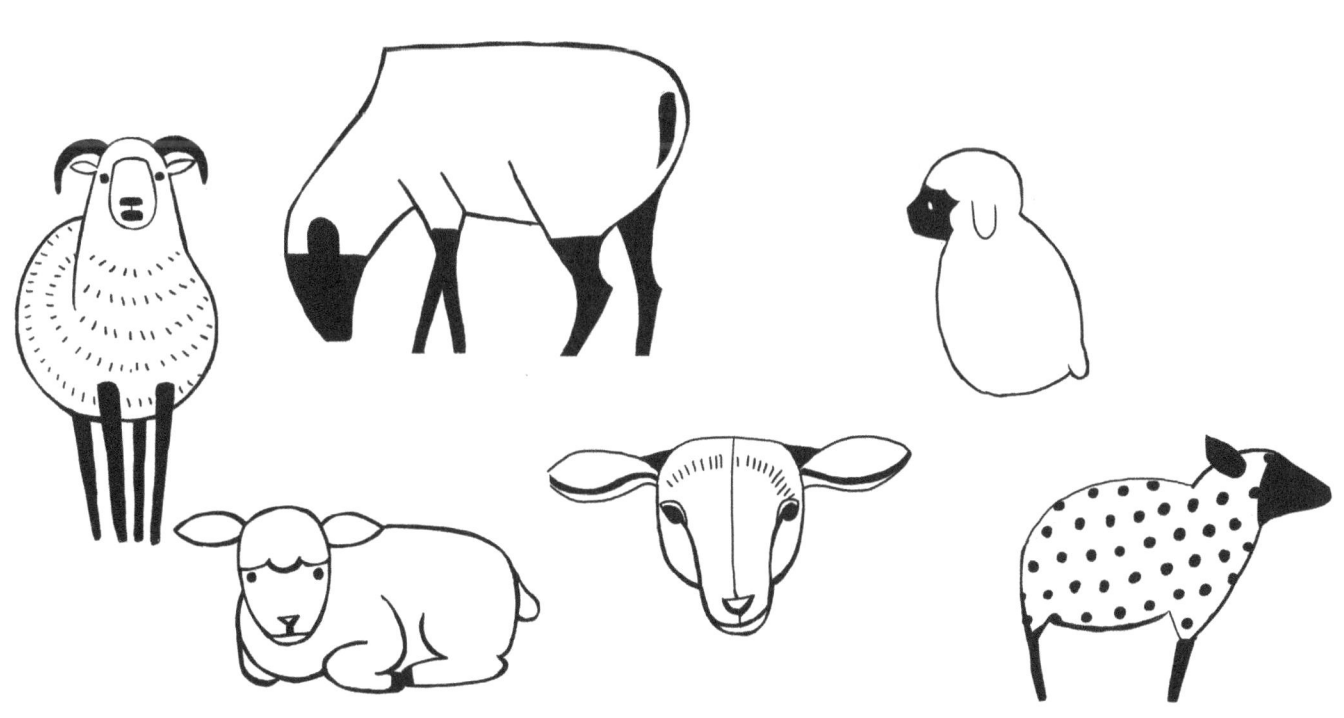

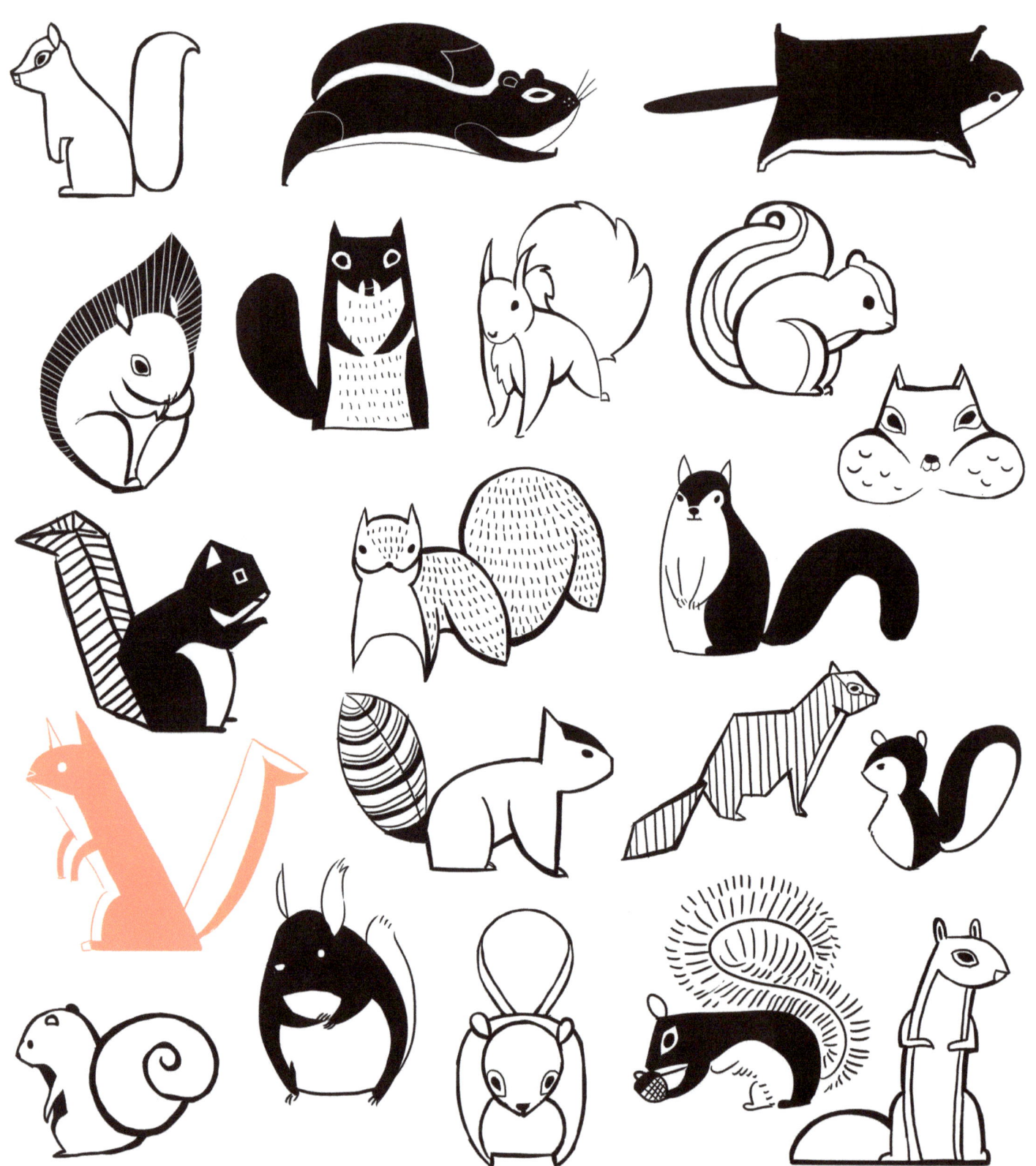

DRAW 20 SQUIRRELS

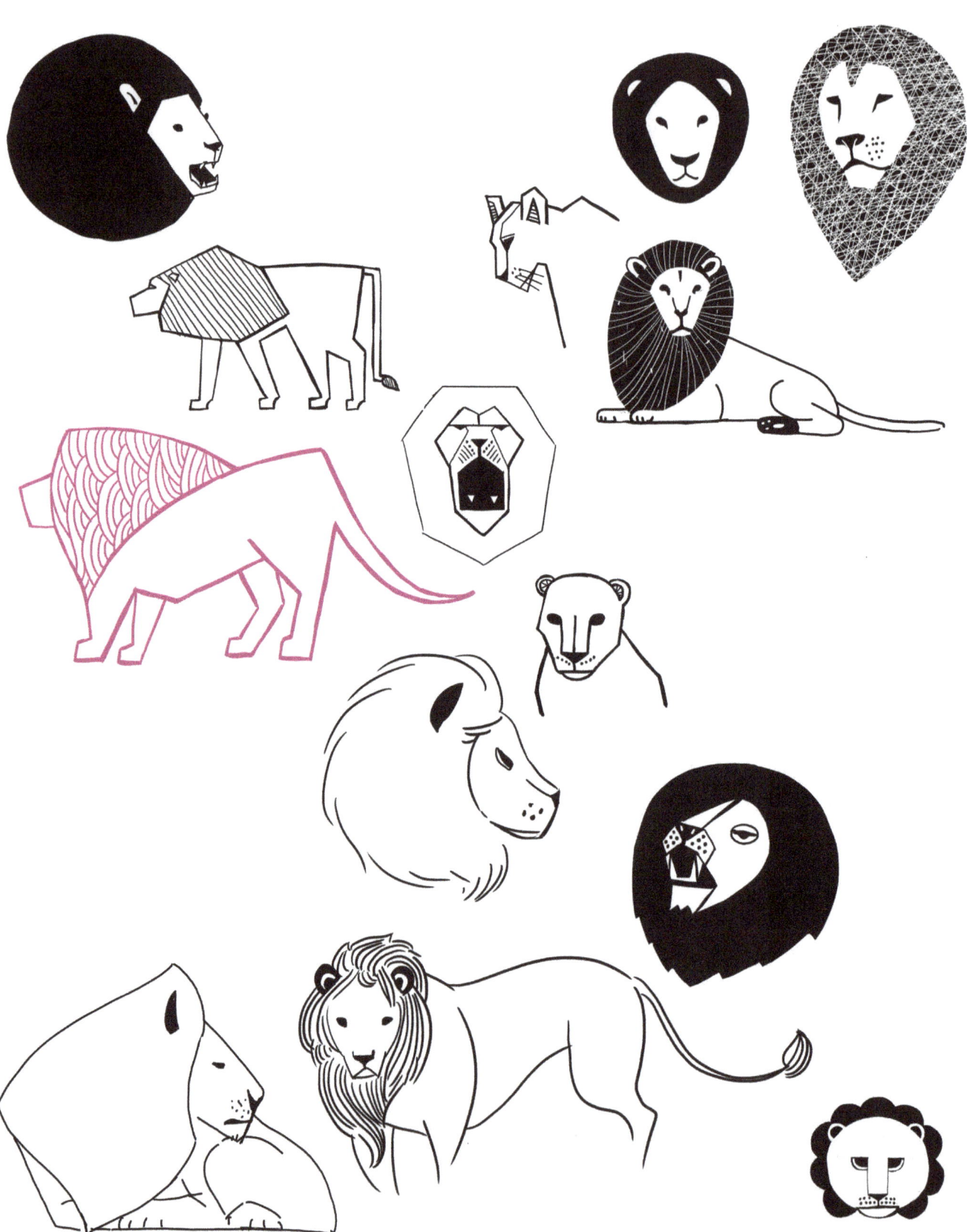

DRAW 20
LIONS

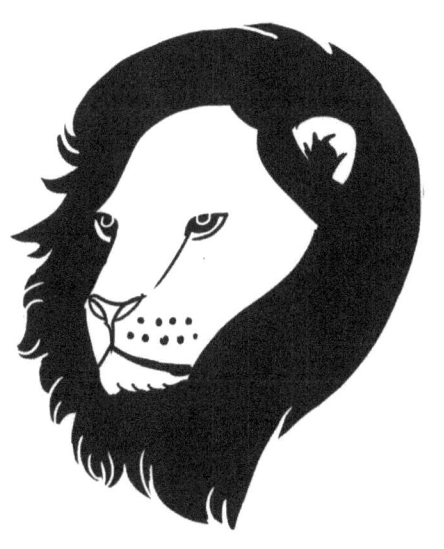

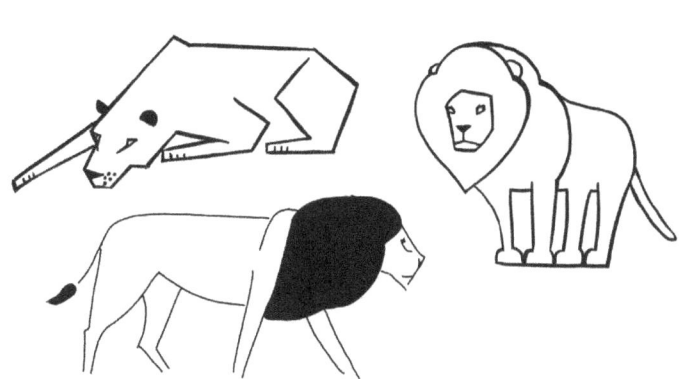

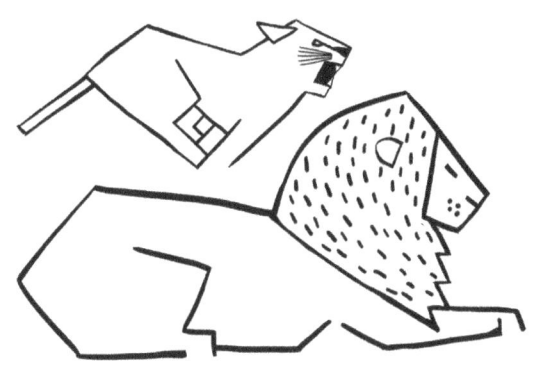

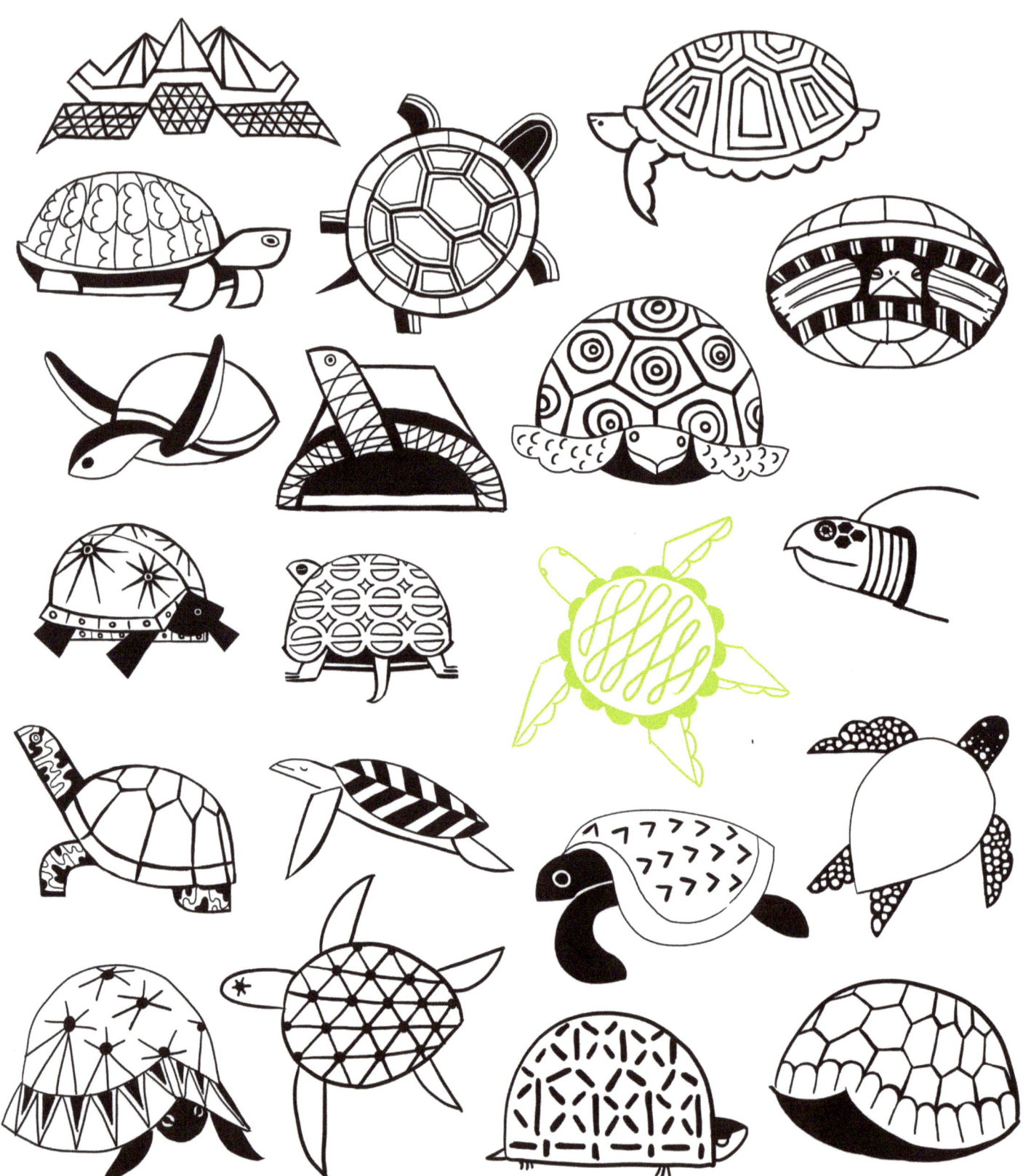

DRAW 20
TURTLES

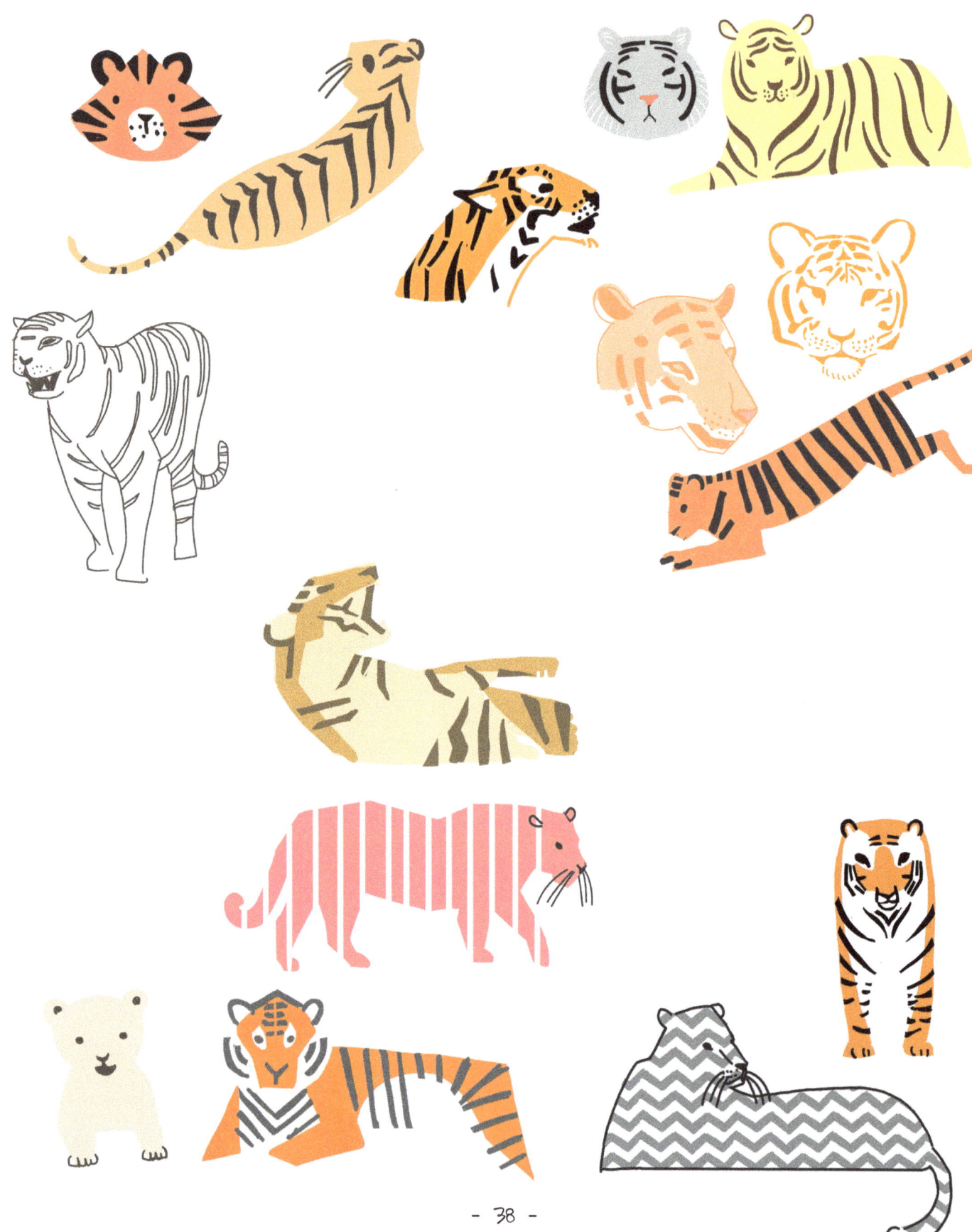

DRAW 20
tigers

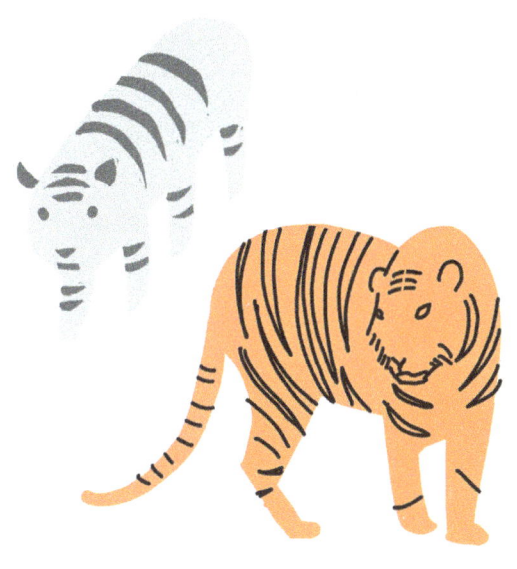
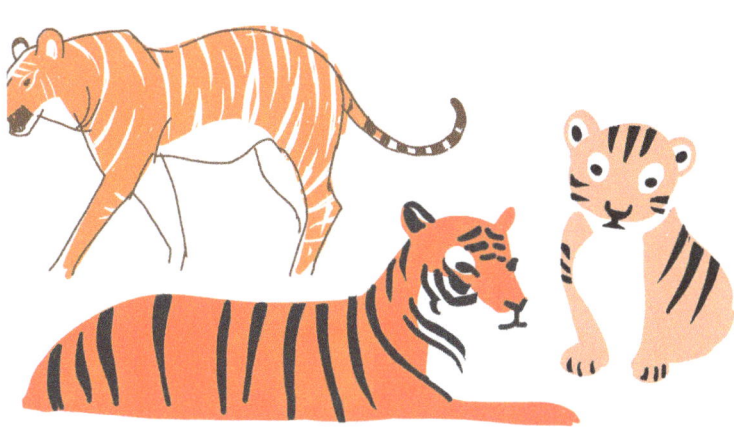

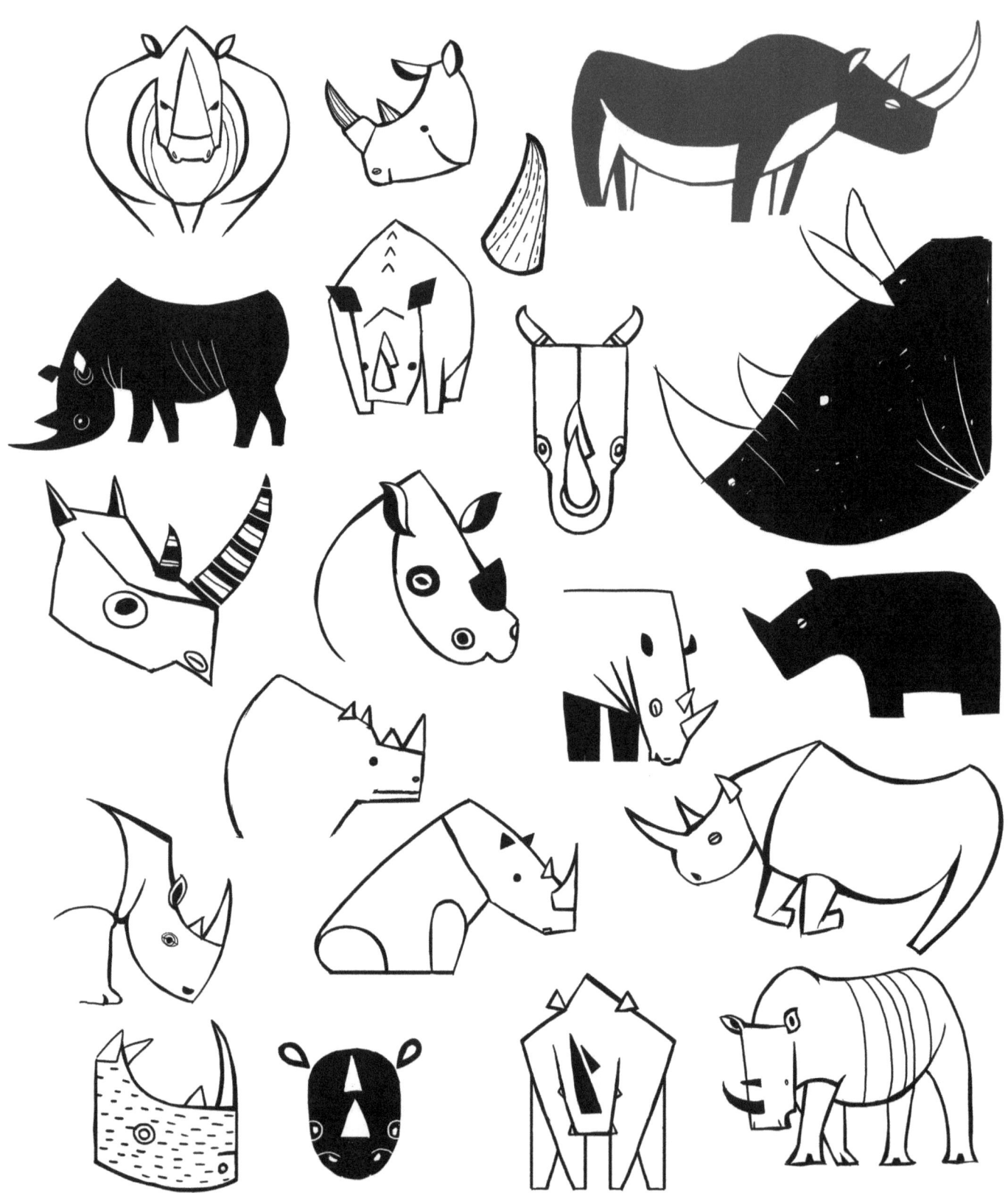

DRAW 20 RHINOCEROSES

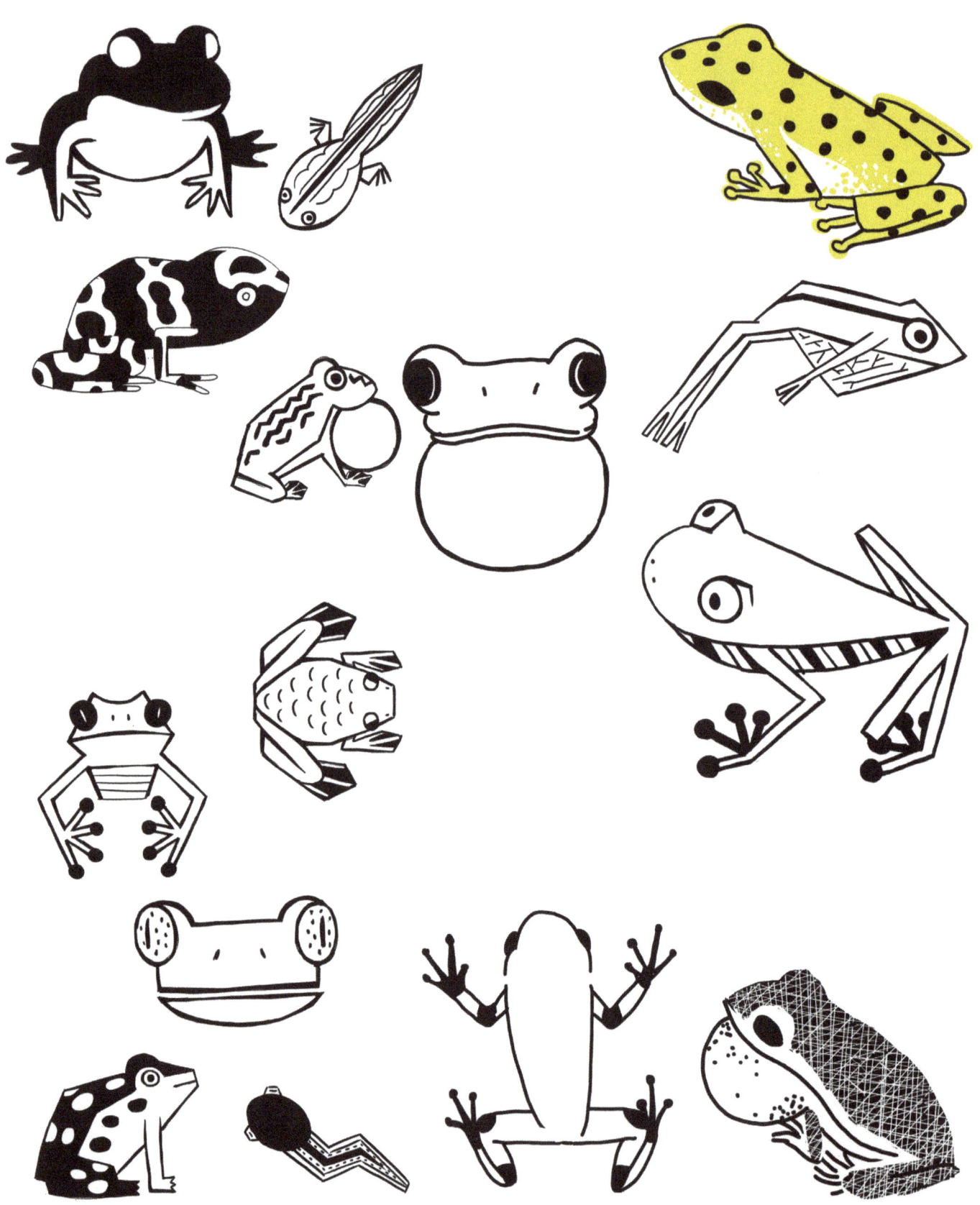

DRAW 20 frogs

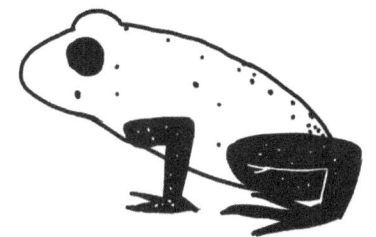
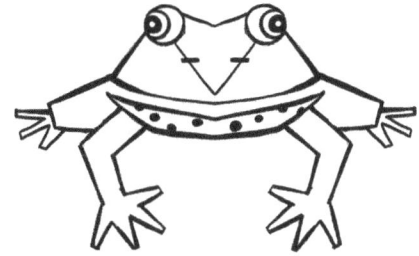
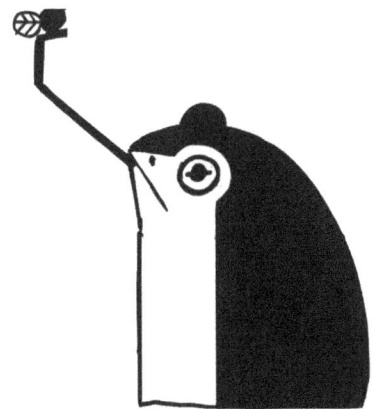
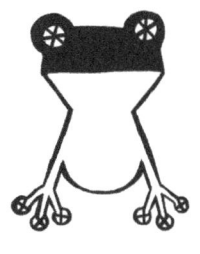
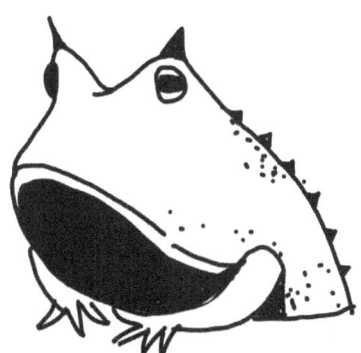

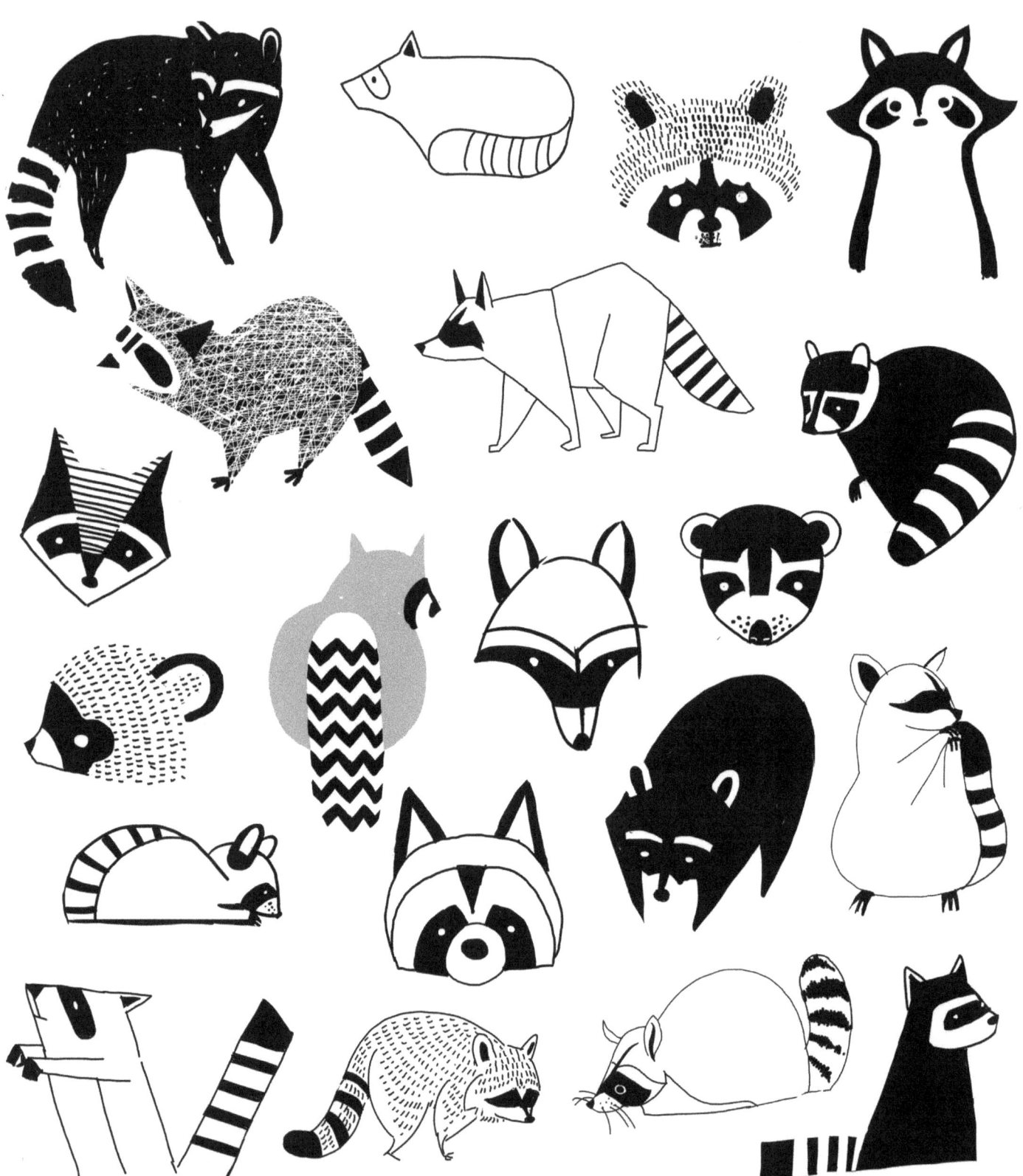

DRAW 20
Raccoons

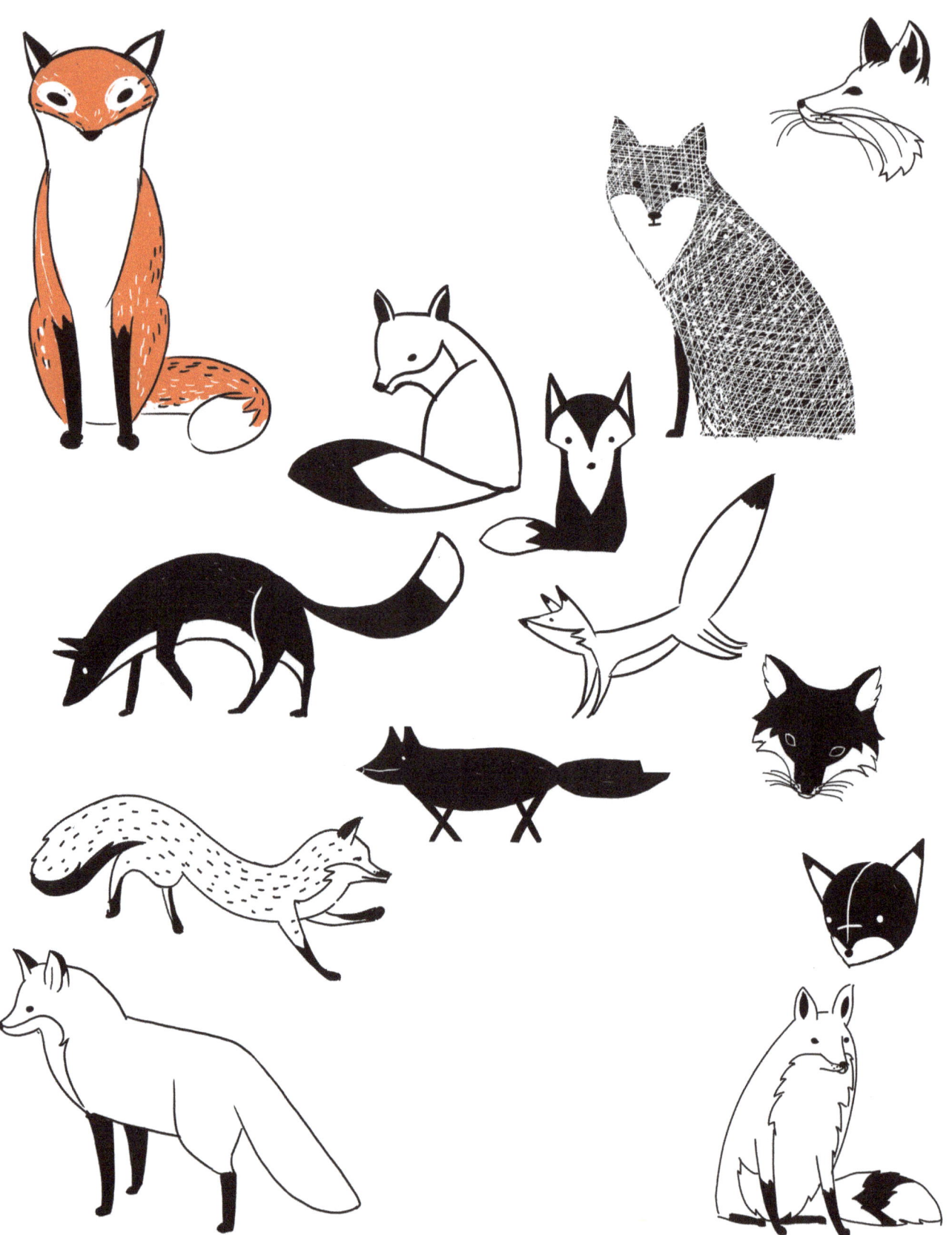

DRAW 20 Foxes

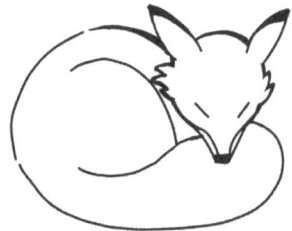
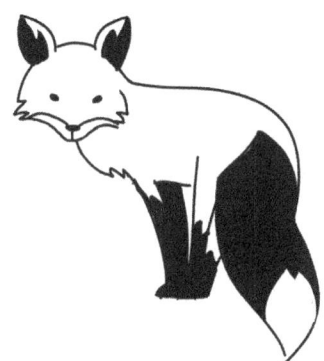
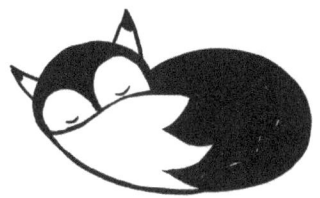
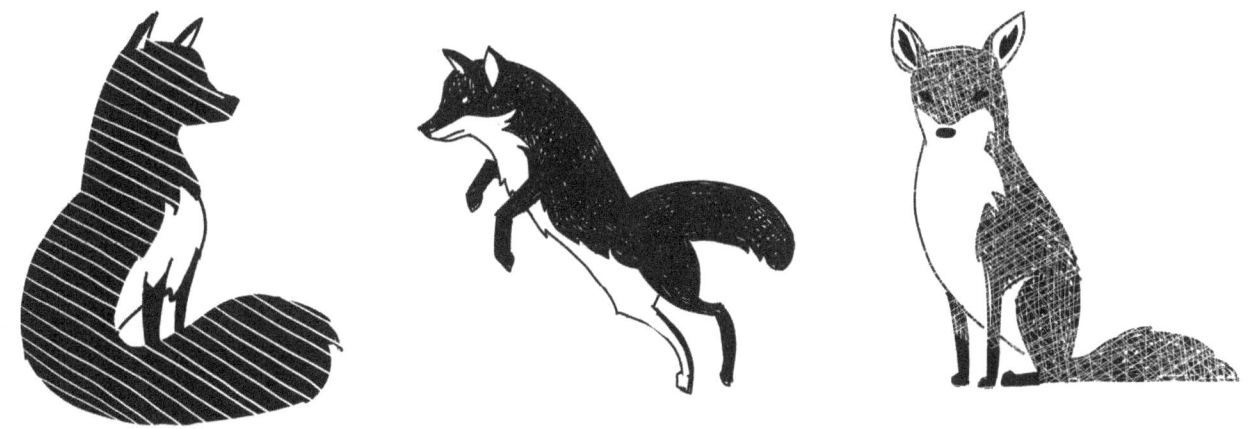

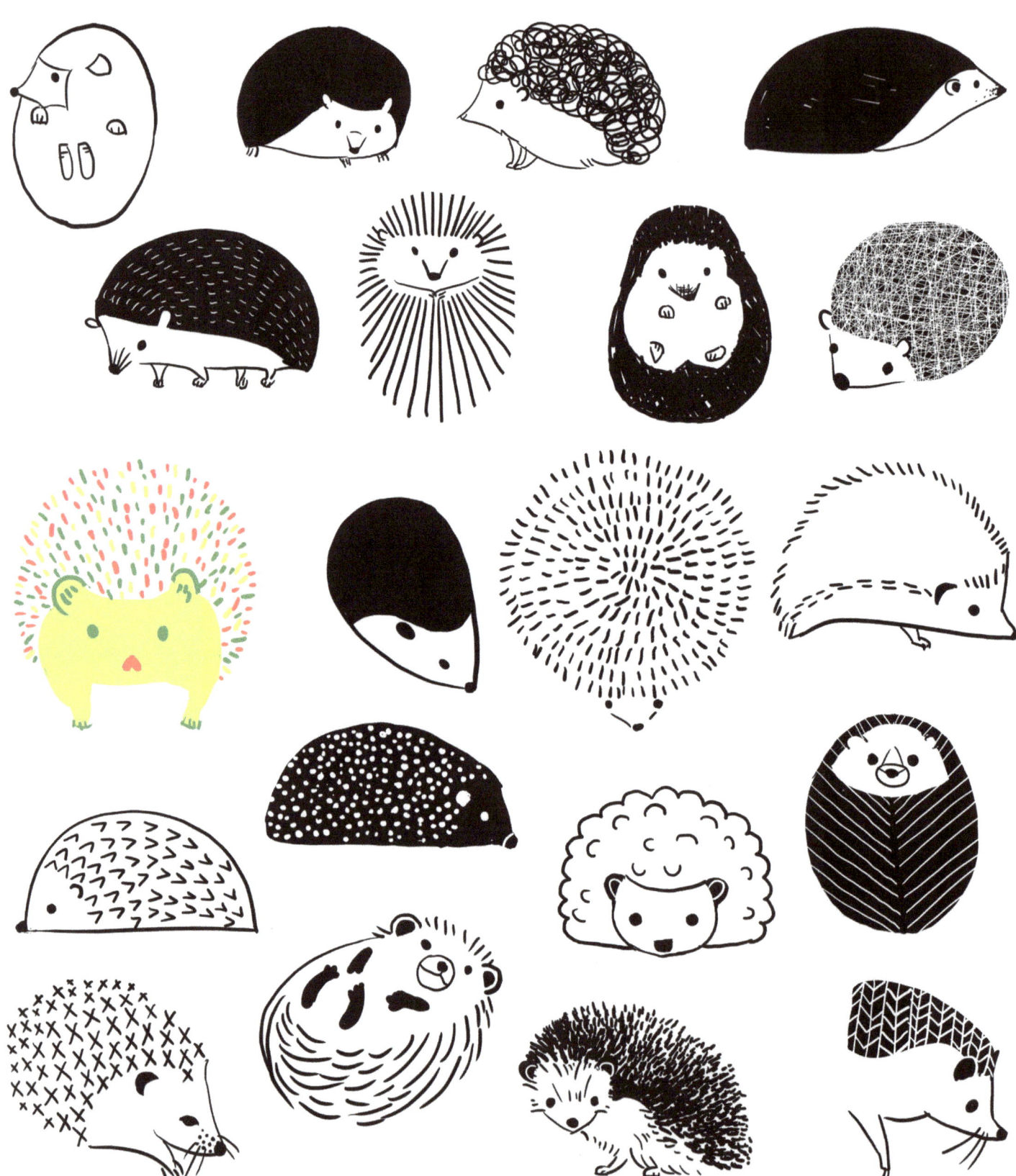

DRAW 20
hedgehogs

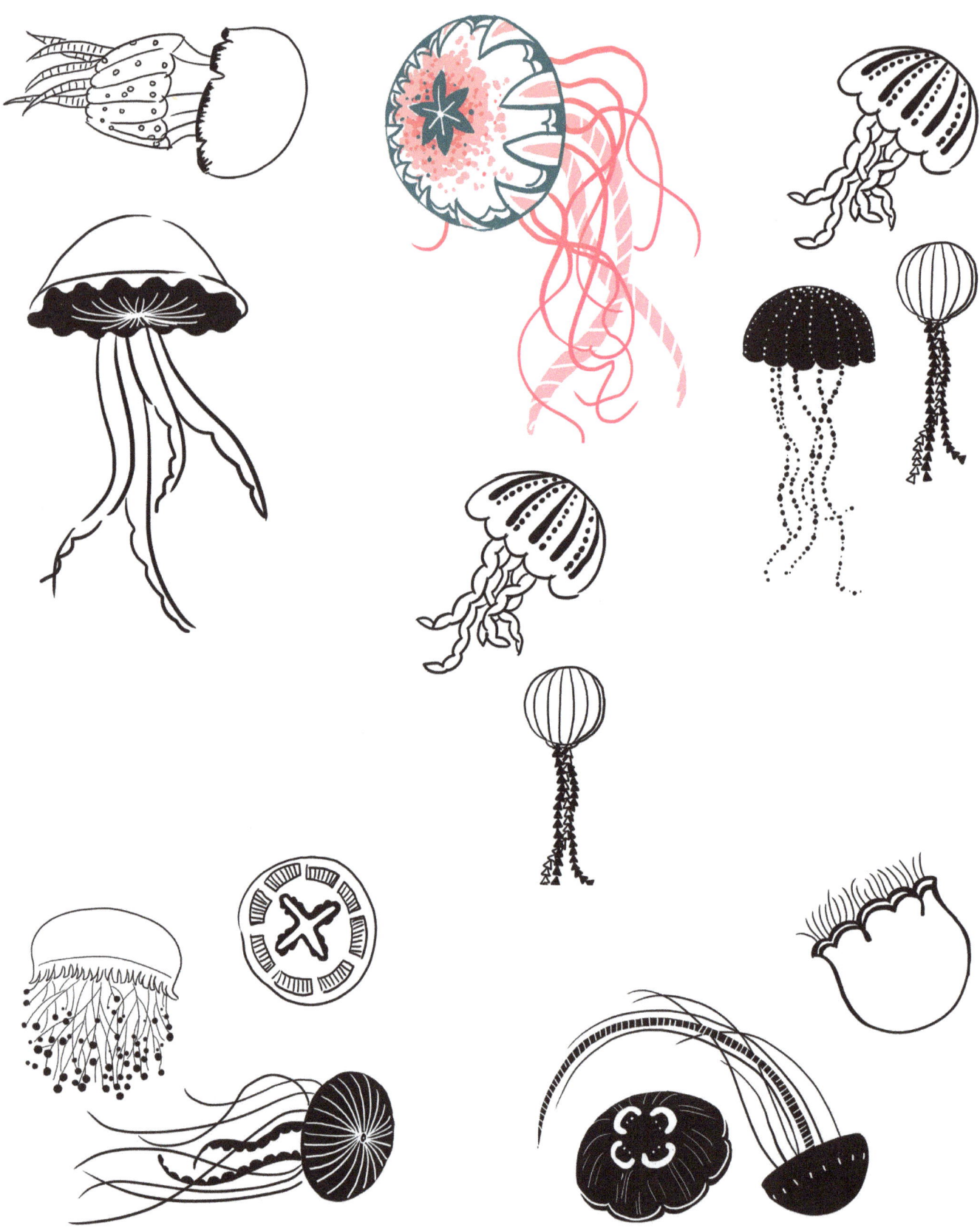

DRAW 20
jellyfish

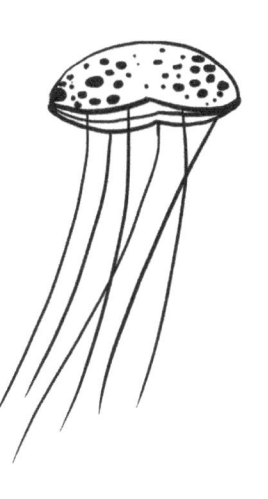
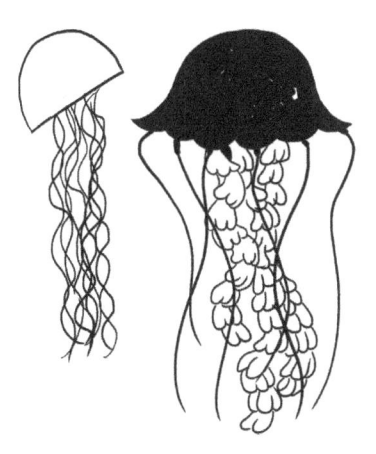
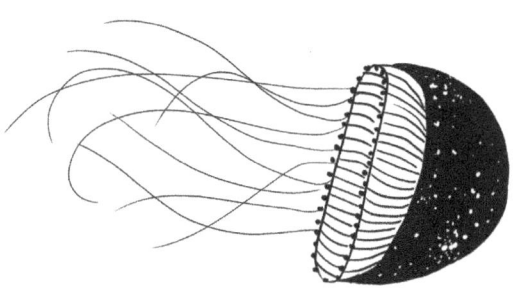
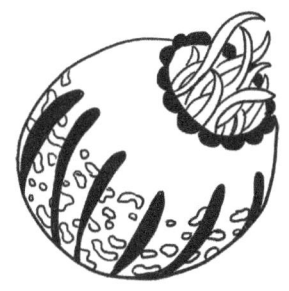

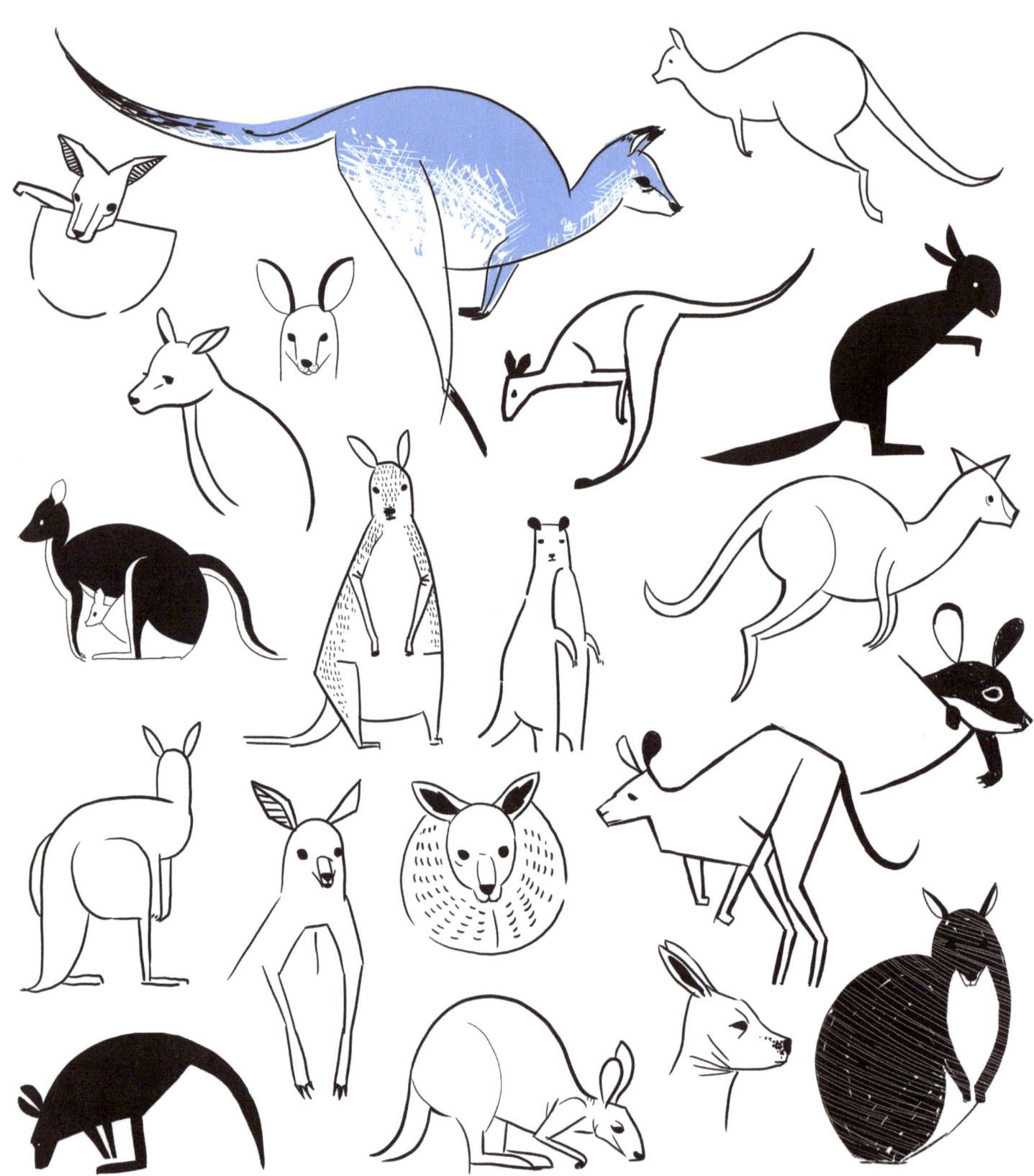

DRAW 20 Kangaroos

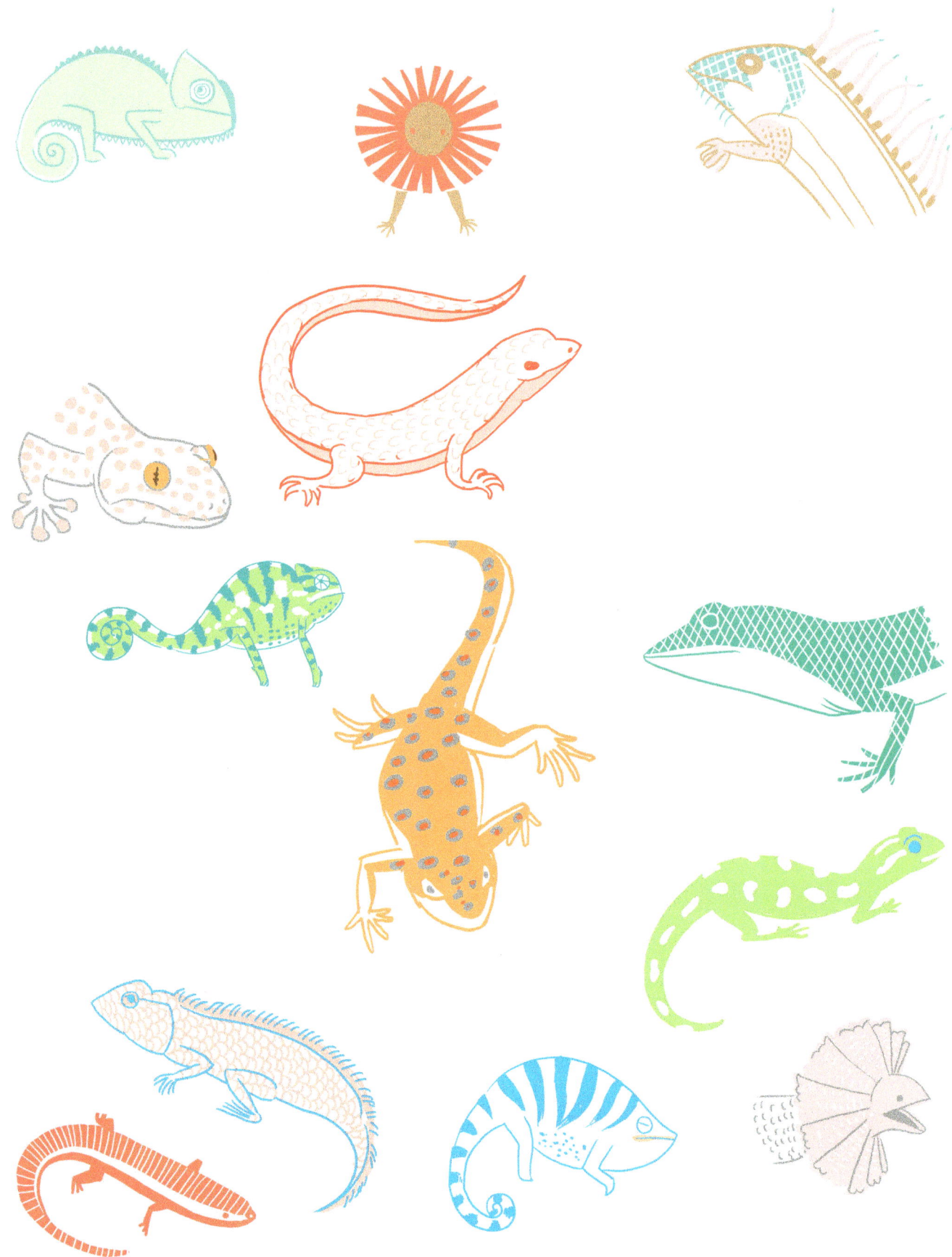

DRAW 20 Lizards

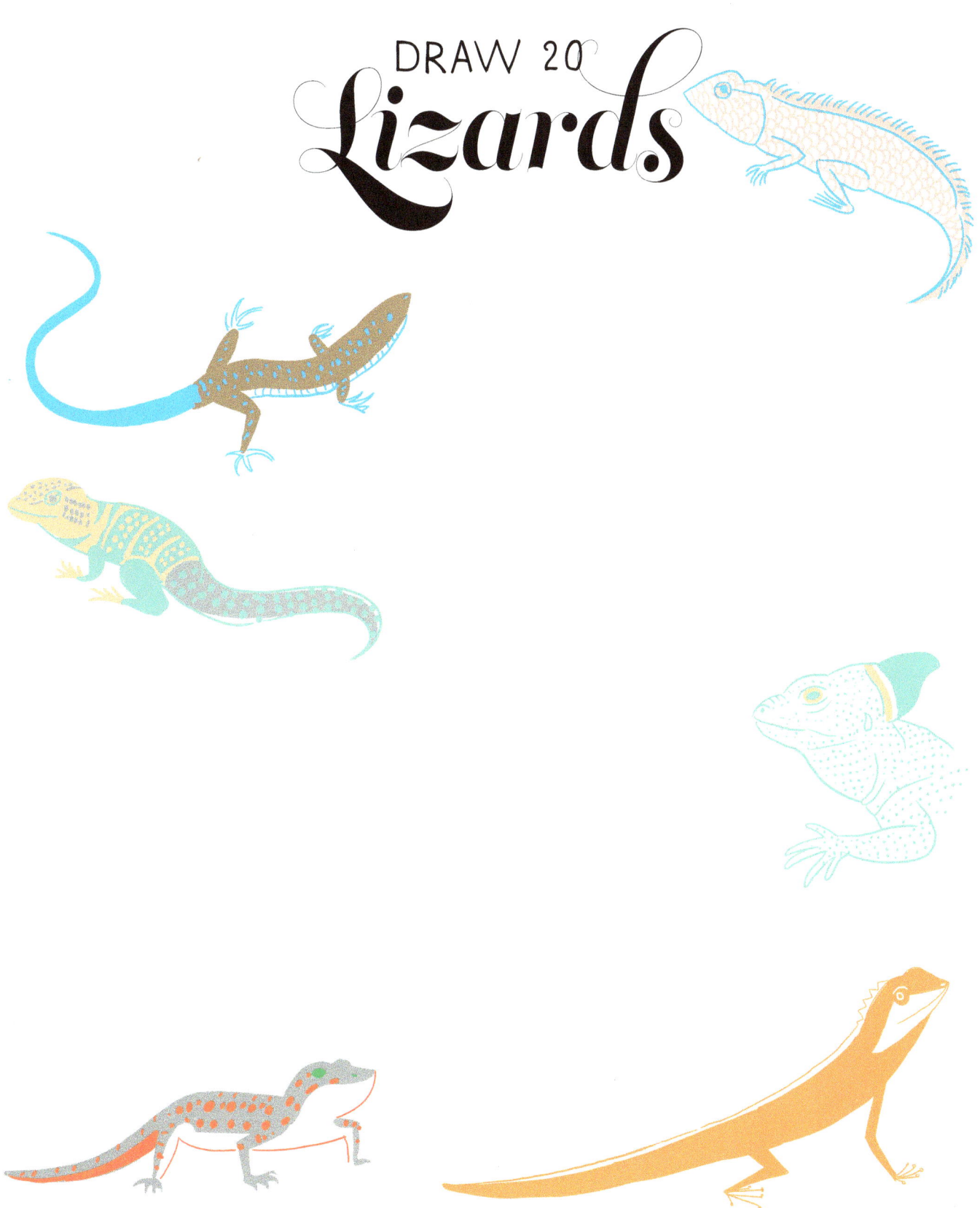

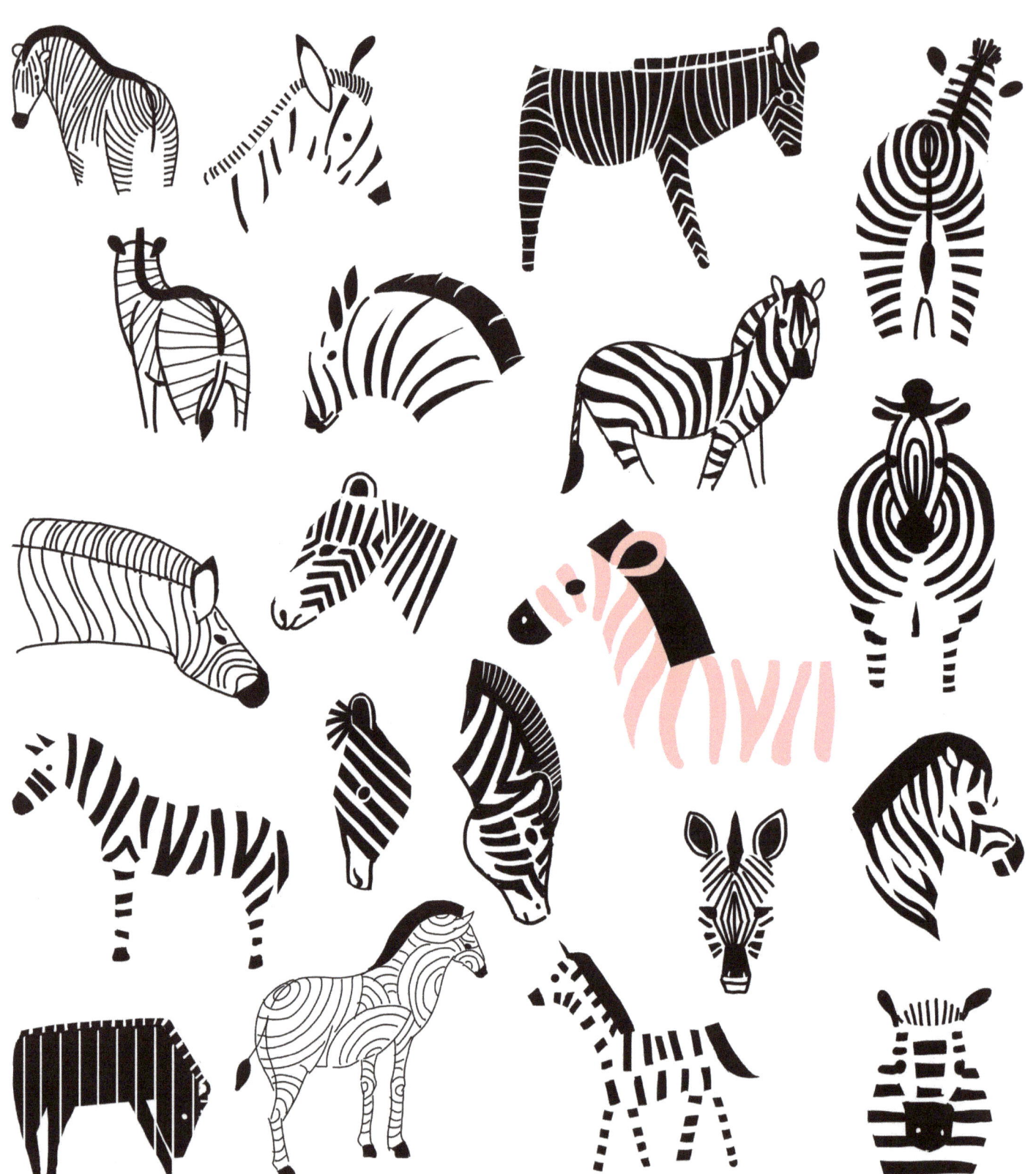

DRAW 20 ZEBRAS

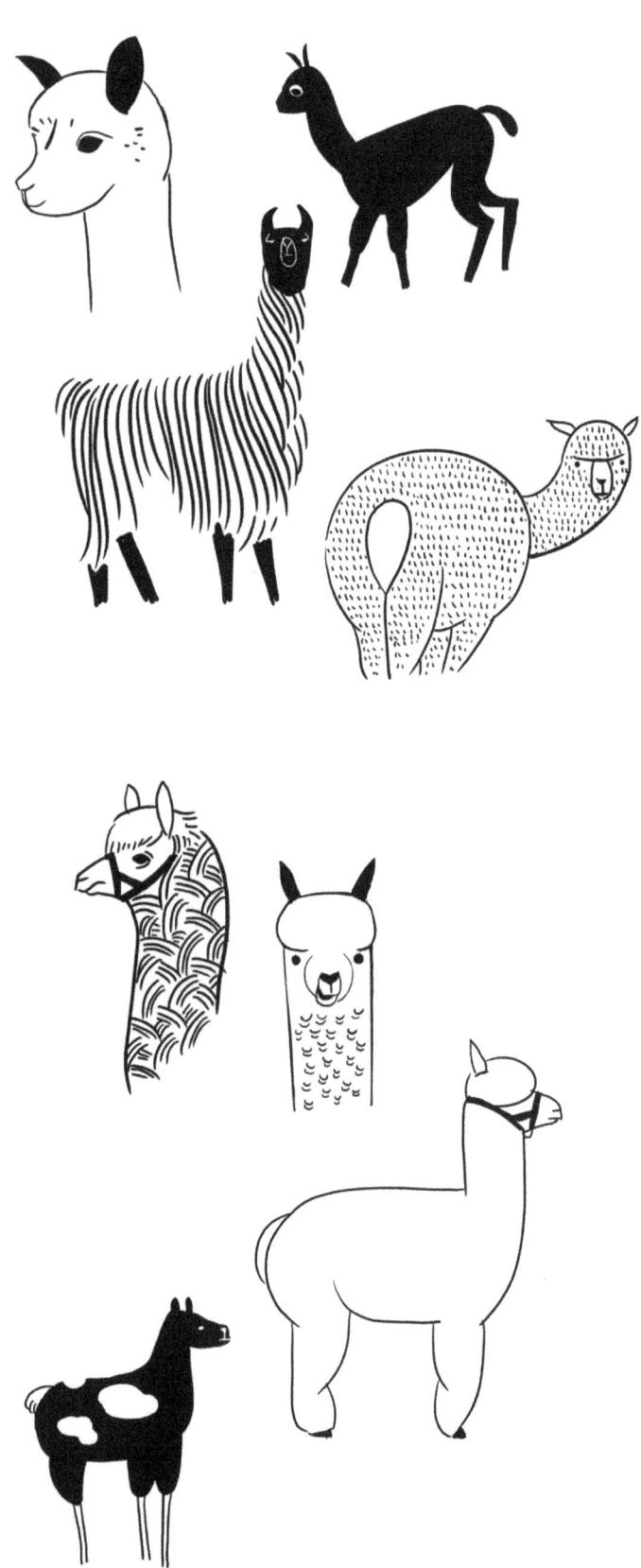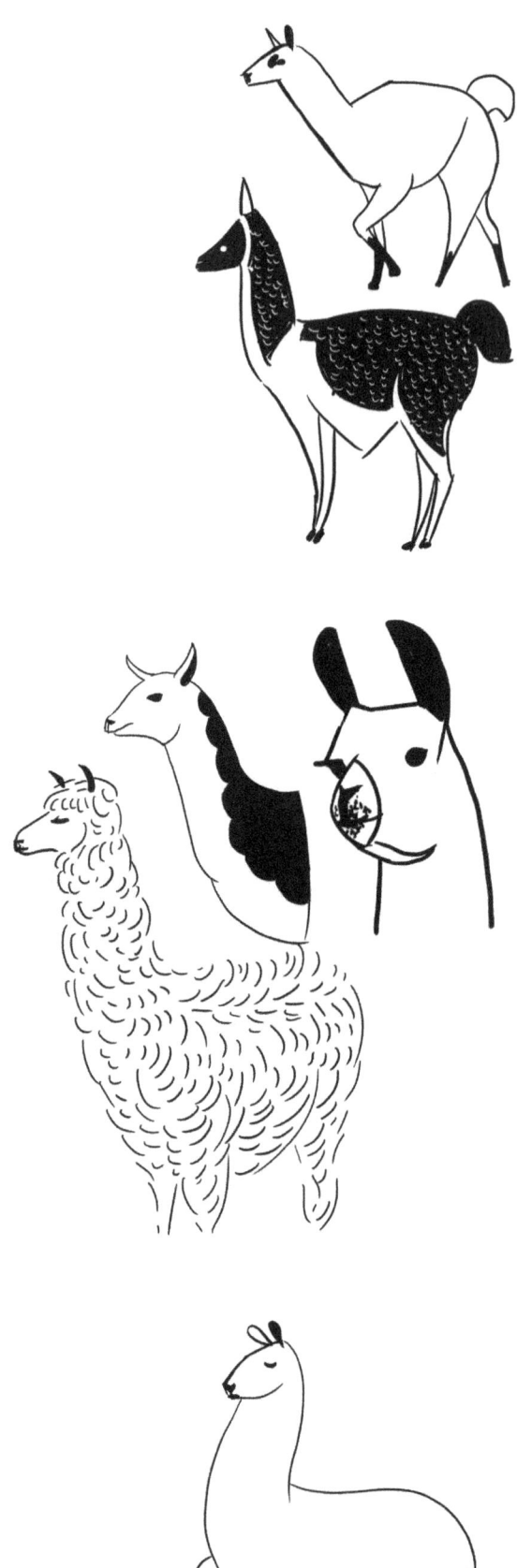

DRAW 20
llamas & alpacas

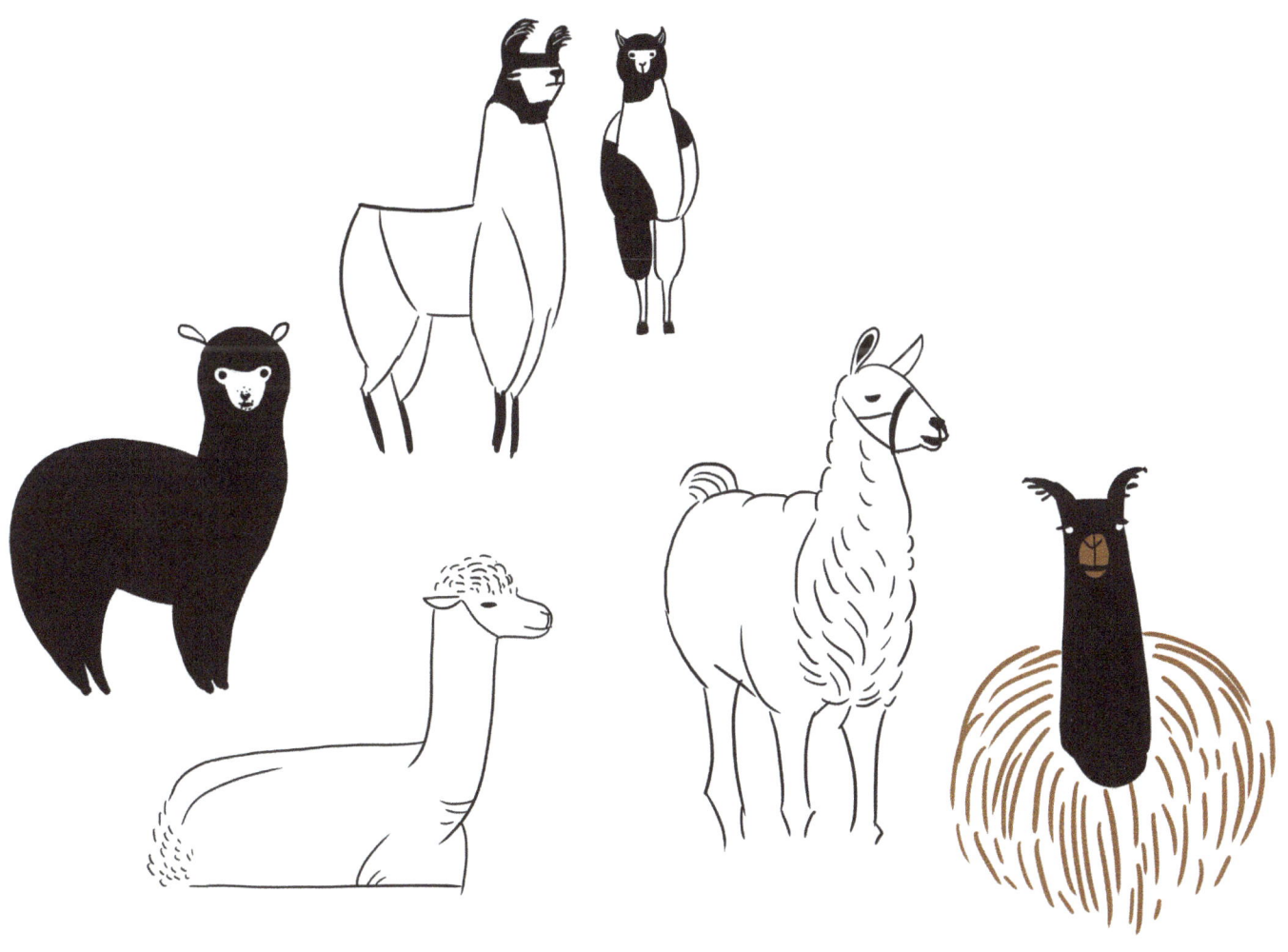

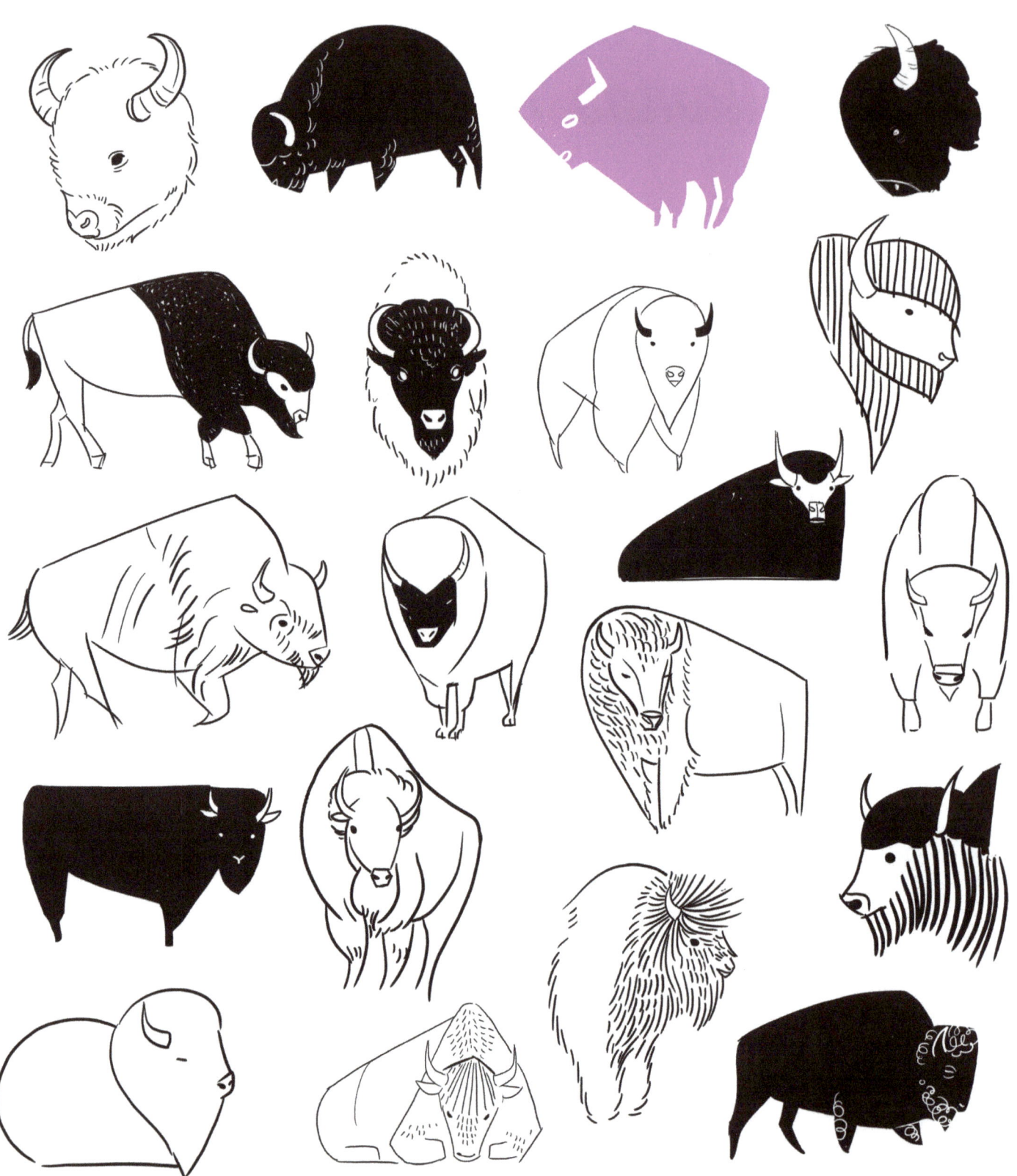

DRAW 20
BUFFALOES

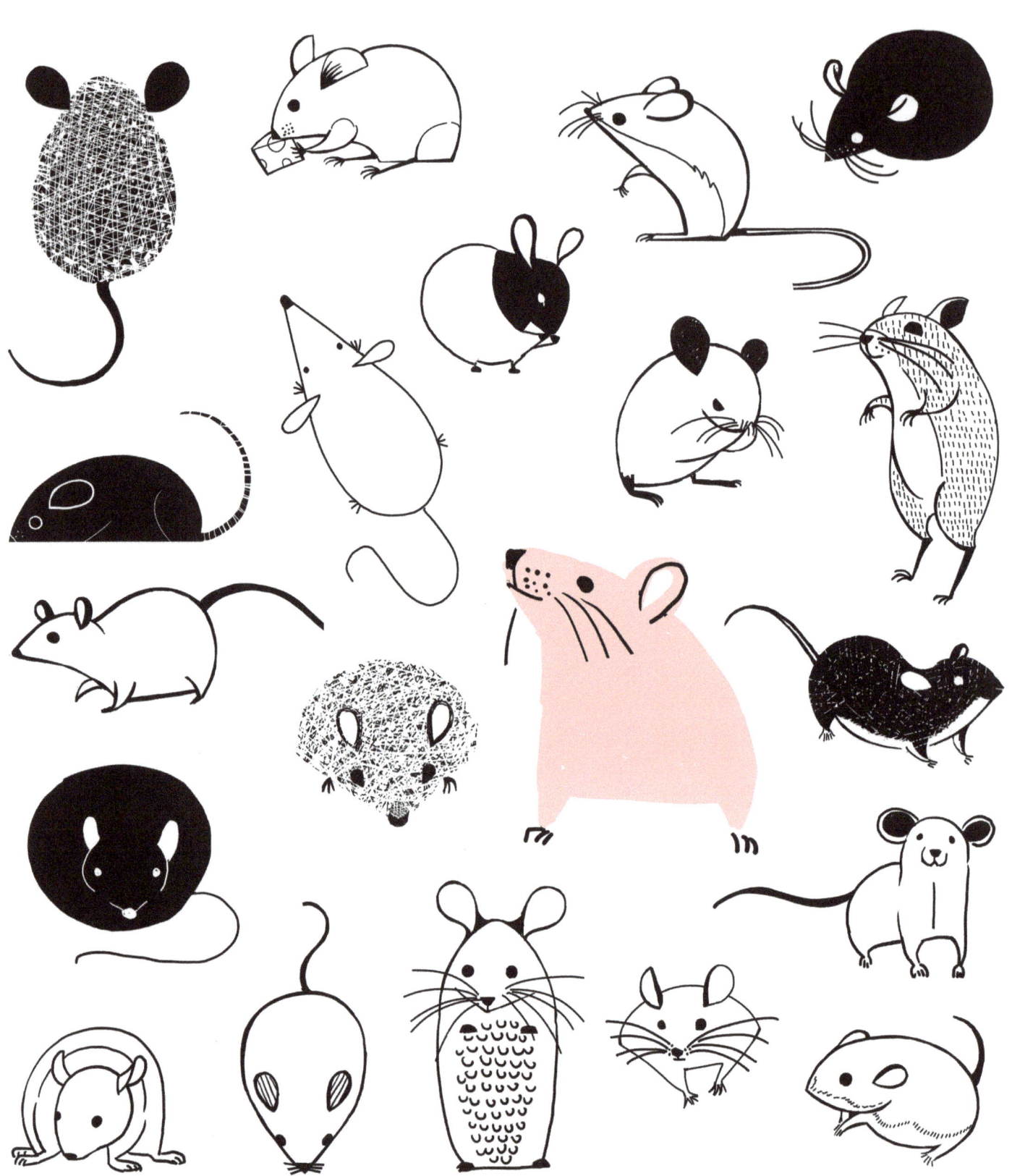

DRAW 20
mice

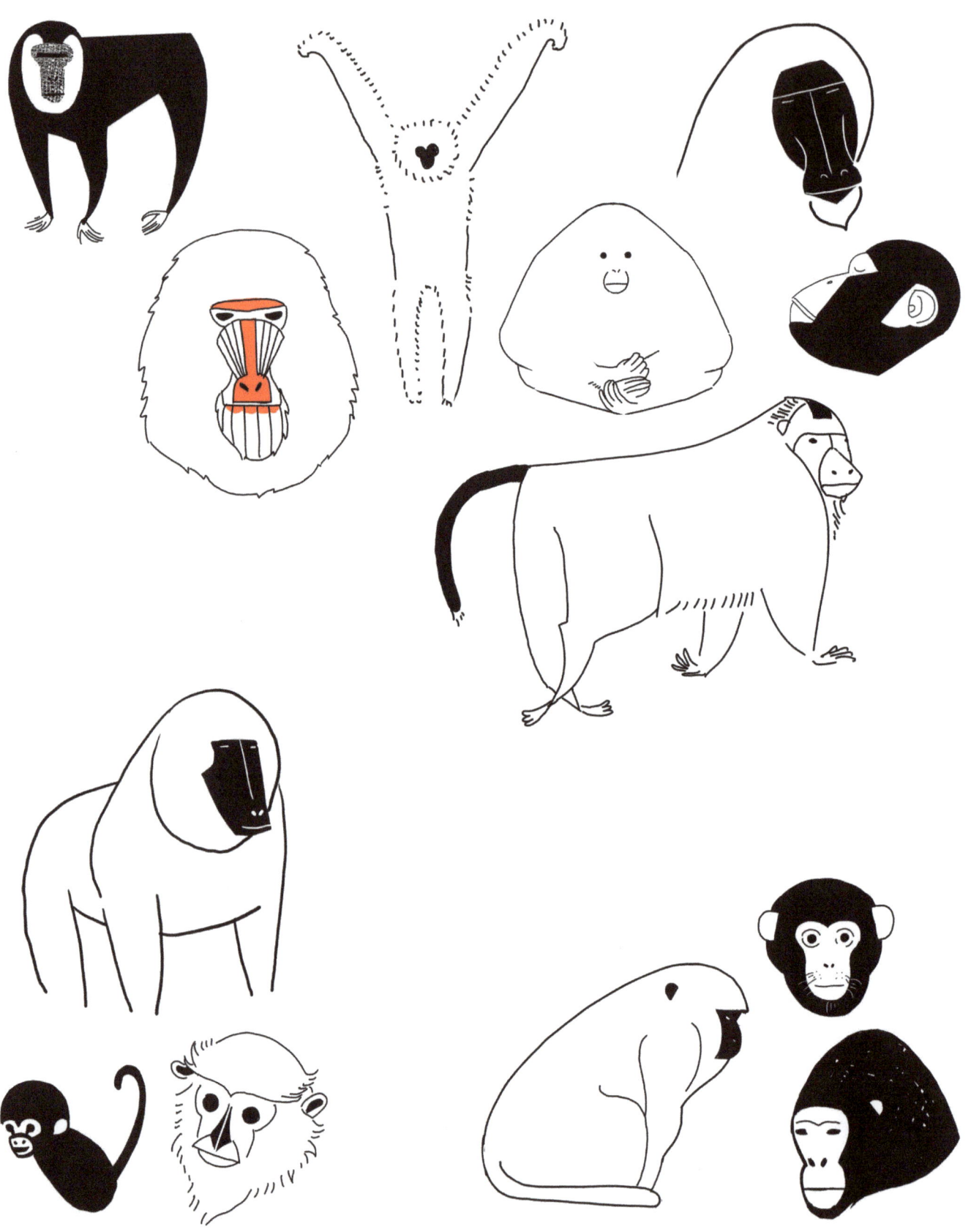

DRAW 20
monkeys & apes

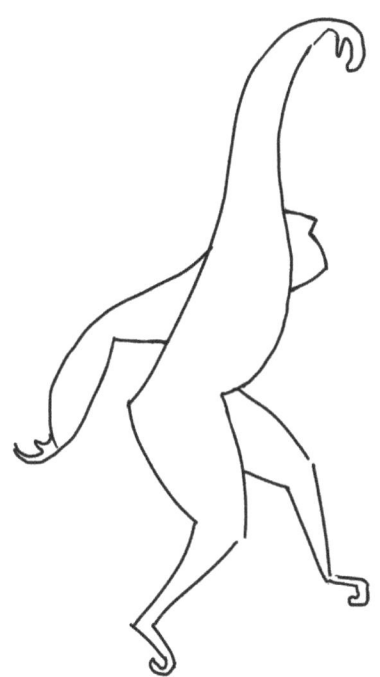
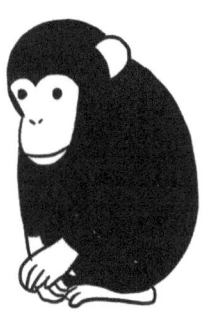
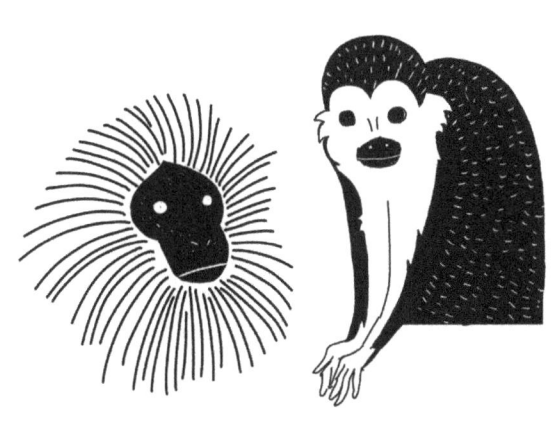
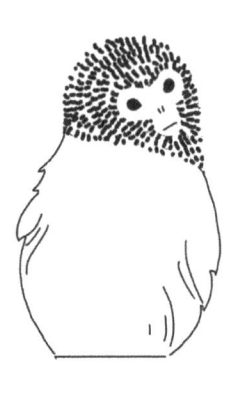
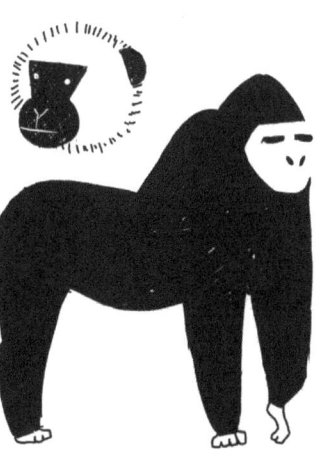

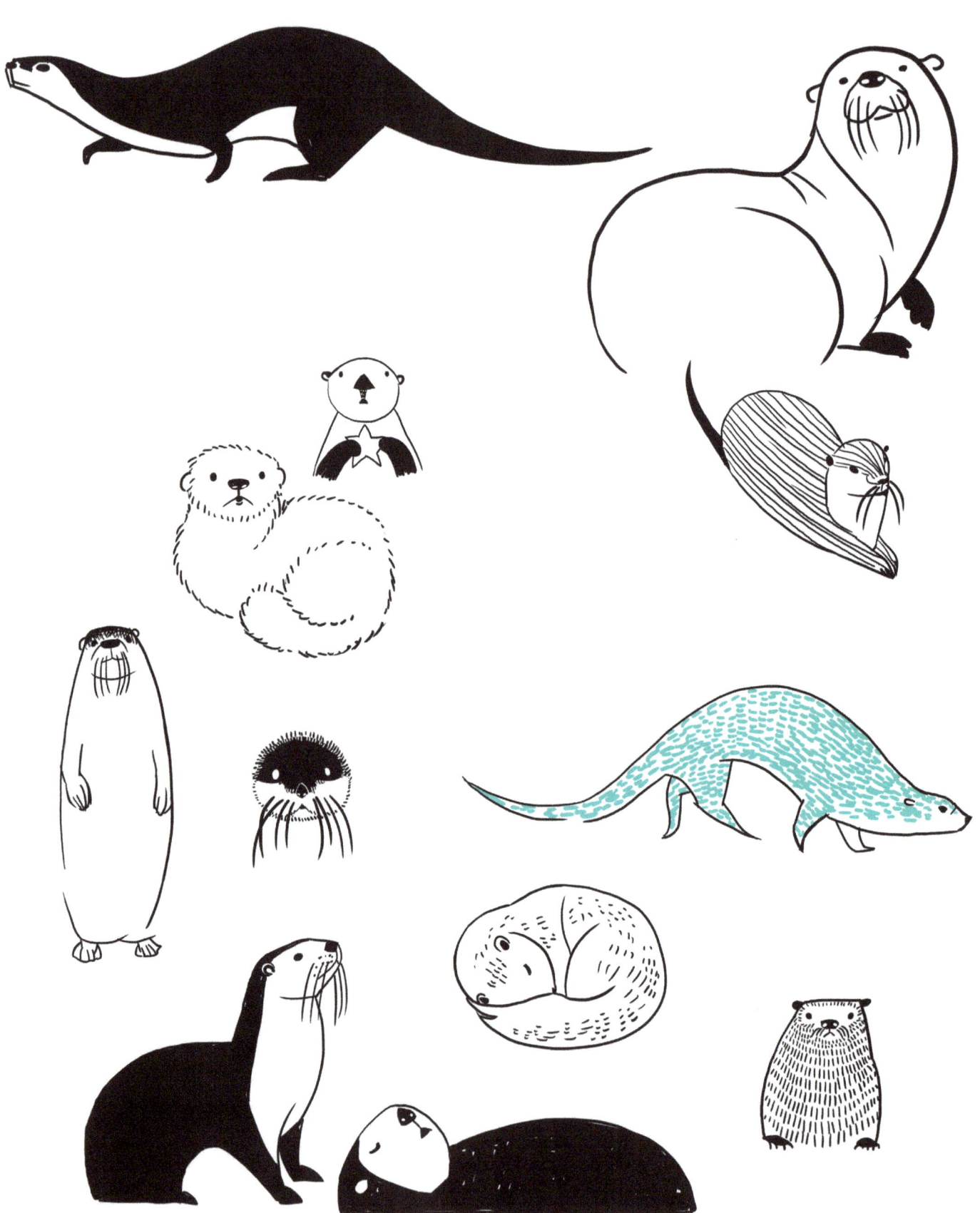

DRAW 20
OTTERS

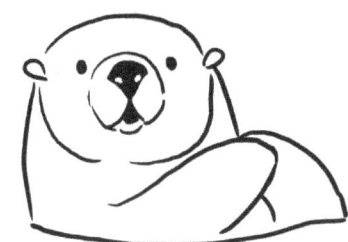
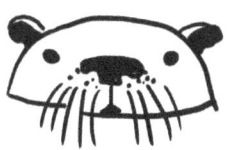
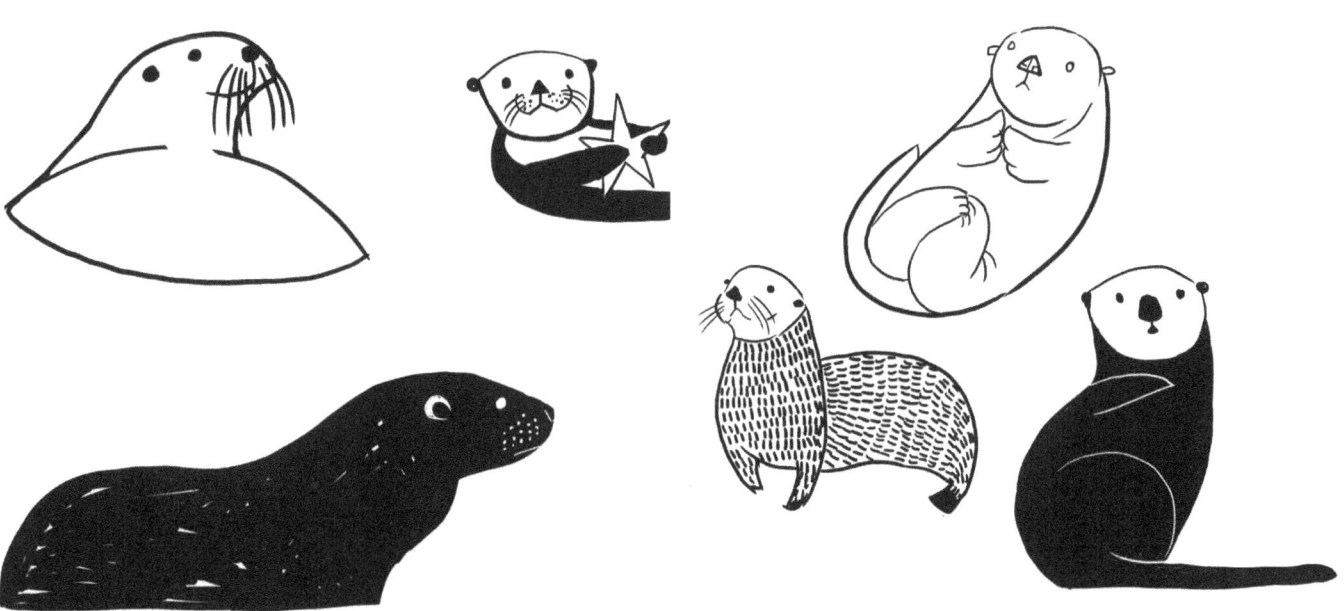

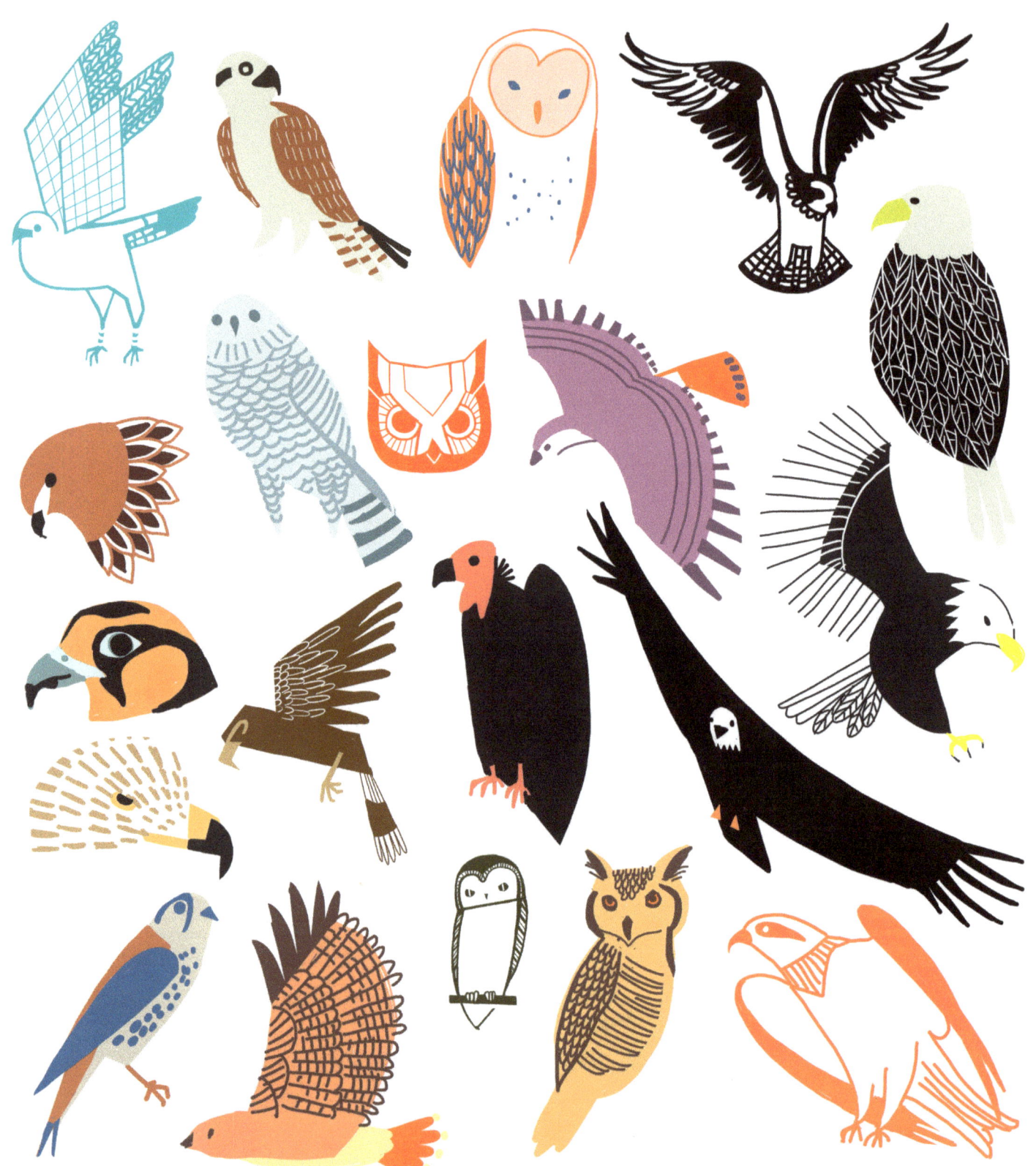

DRAW 20
Birds of Prey

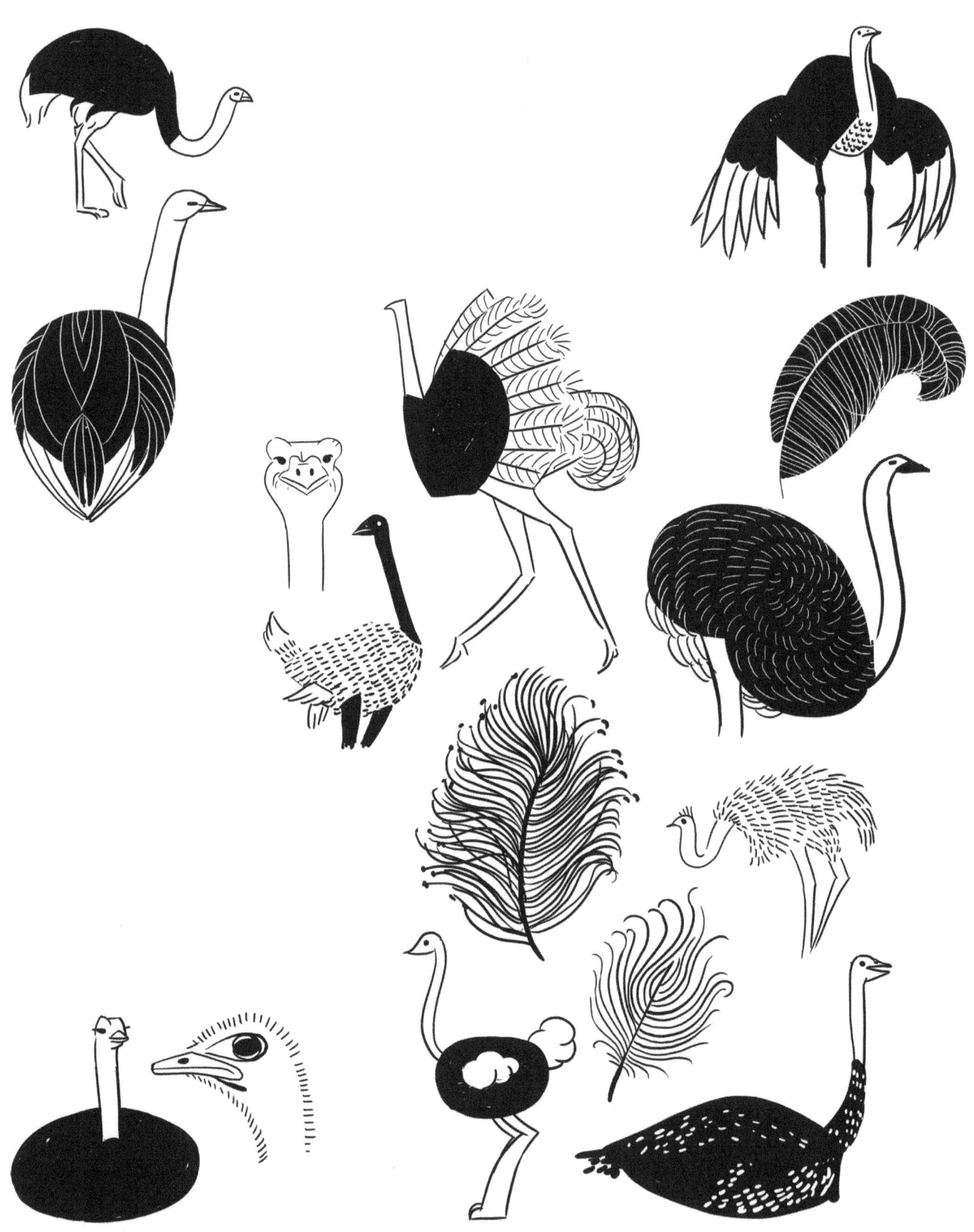

DRAW 20
OSTRICHES

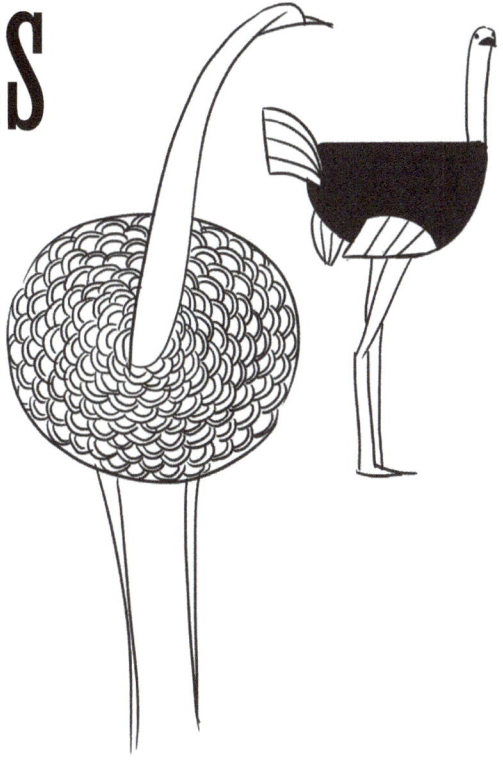
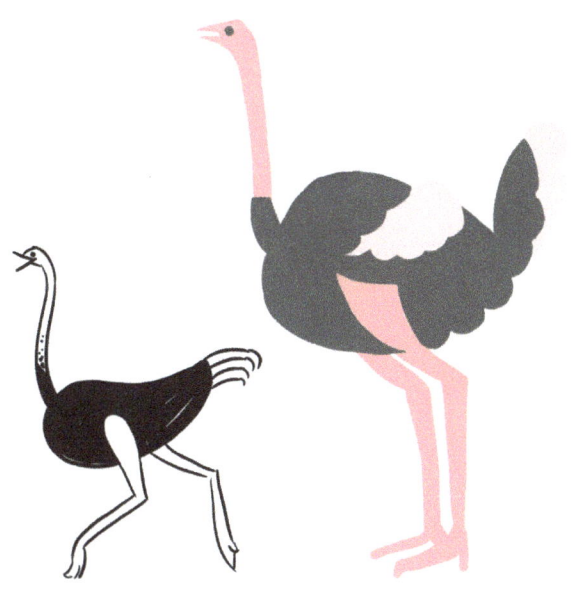
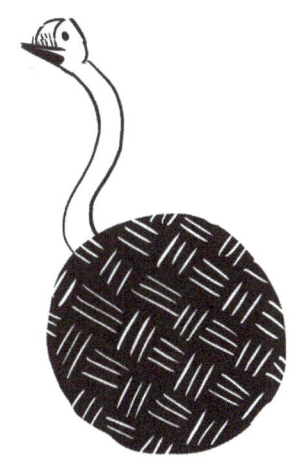

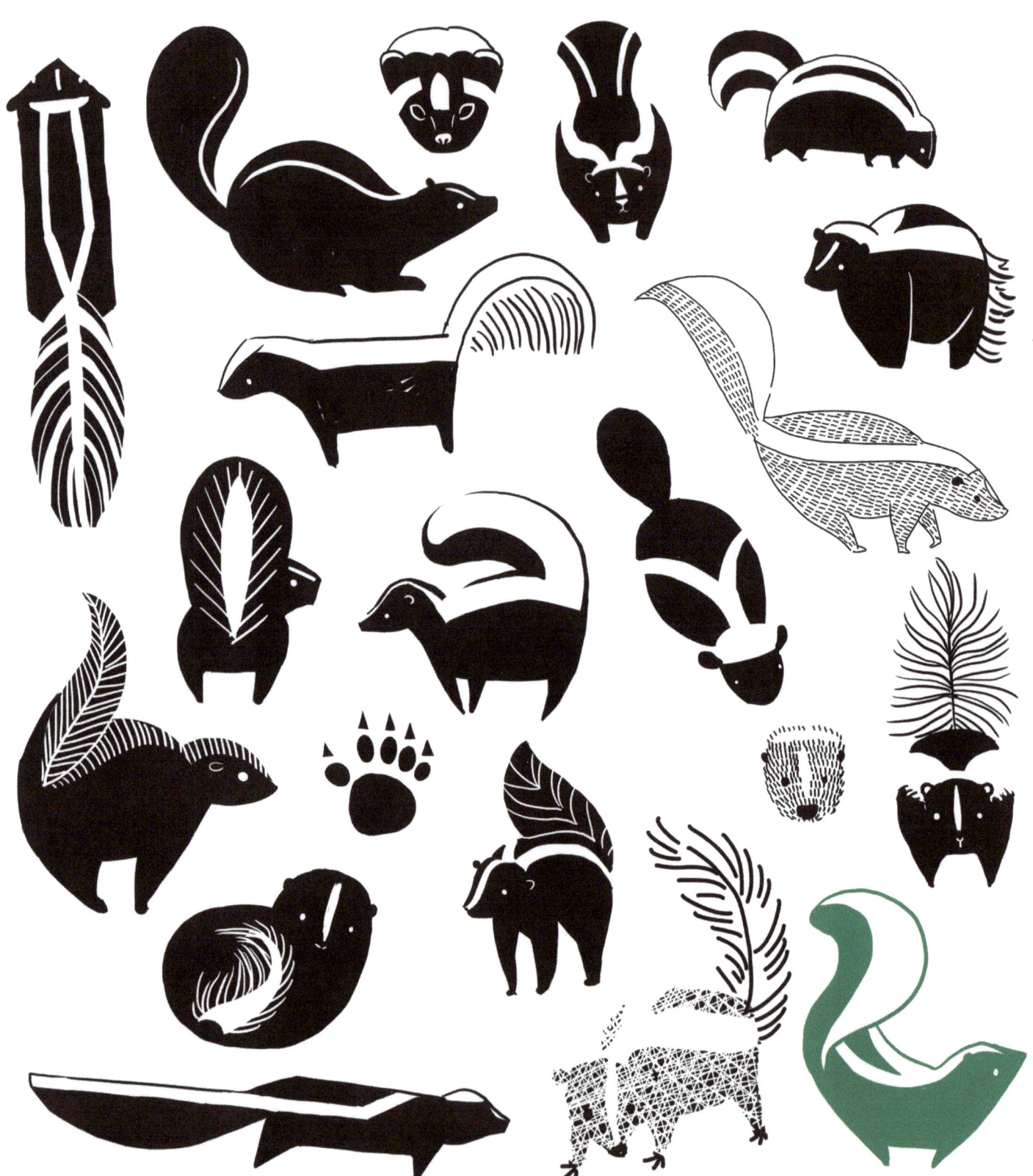

DRAW 20
Skunks

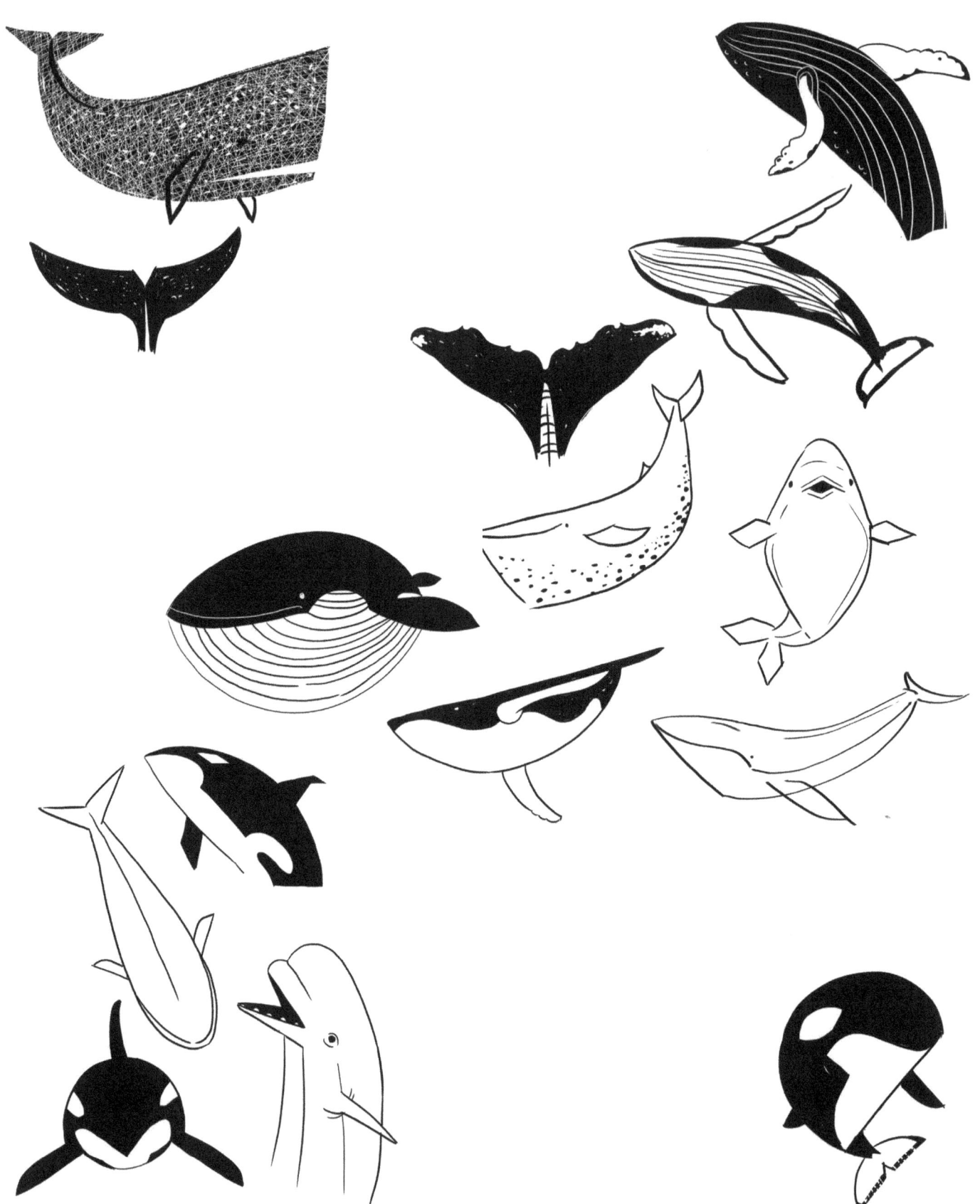

DRAW 20
WHALES

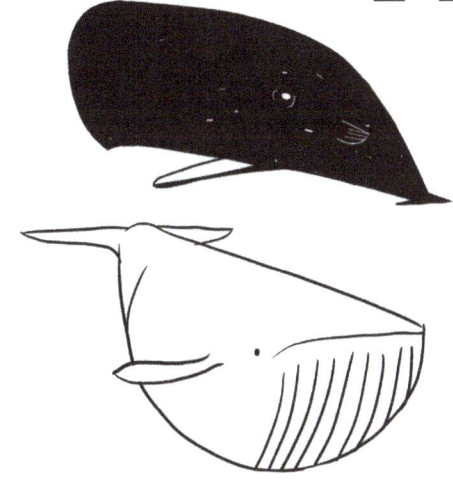
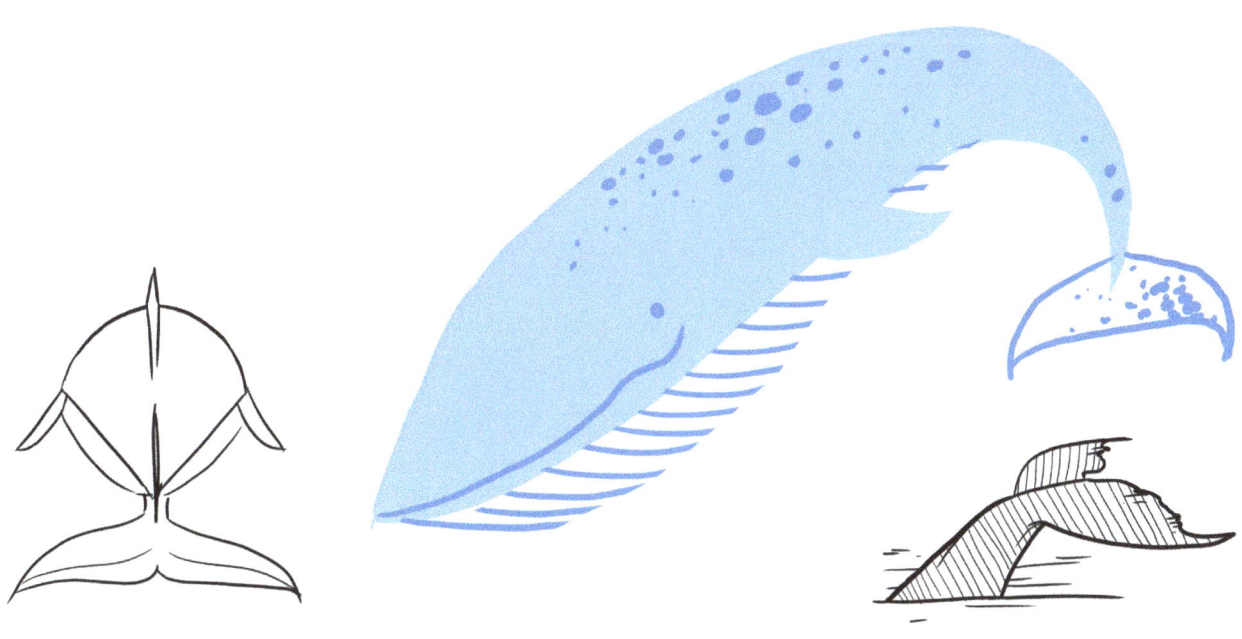

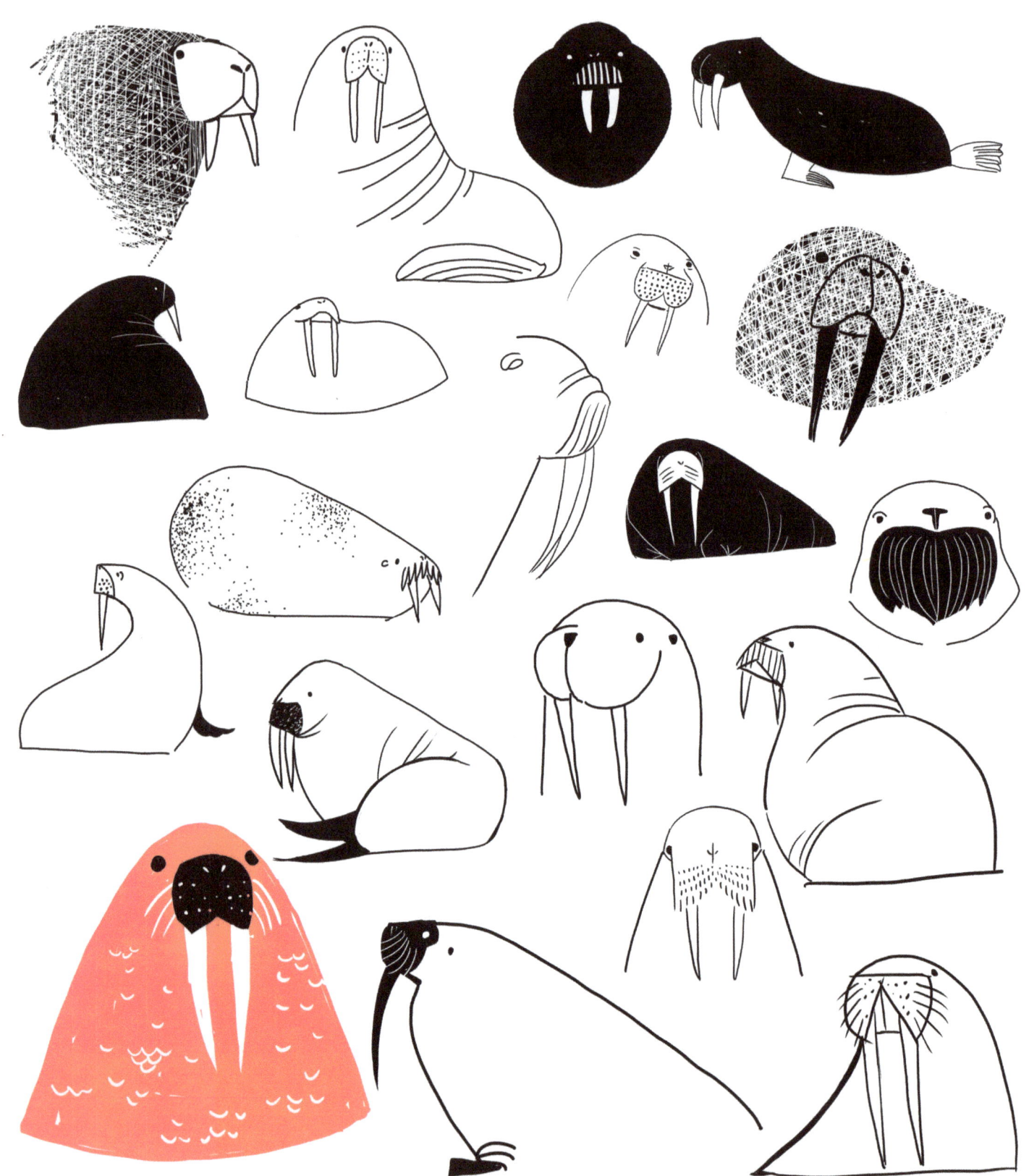

DRAW 20
walruses

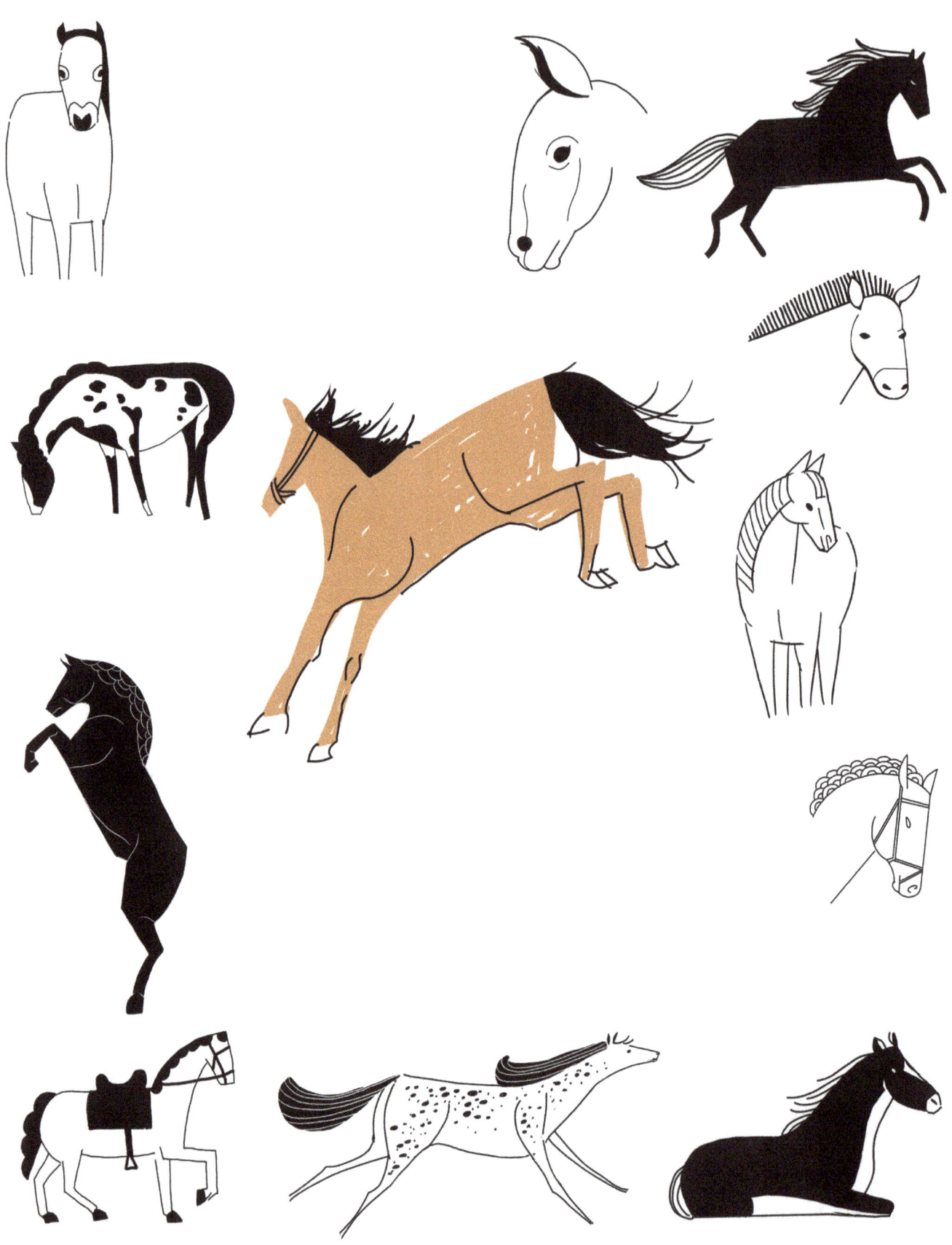

DRAW 20
HORSES

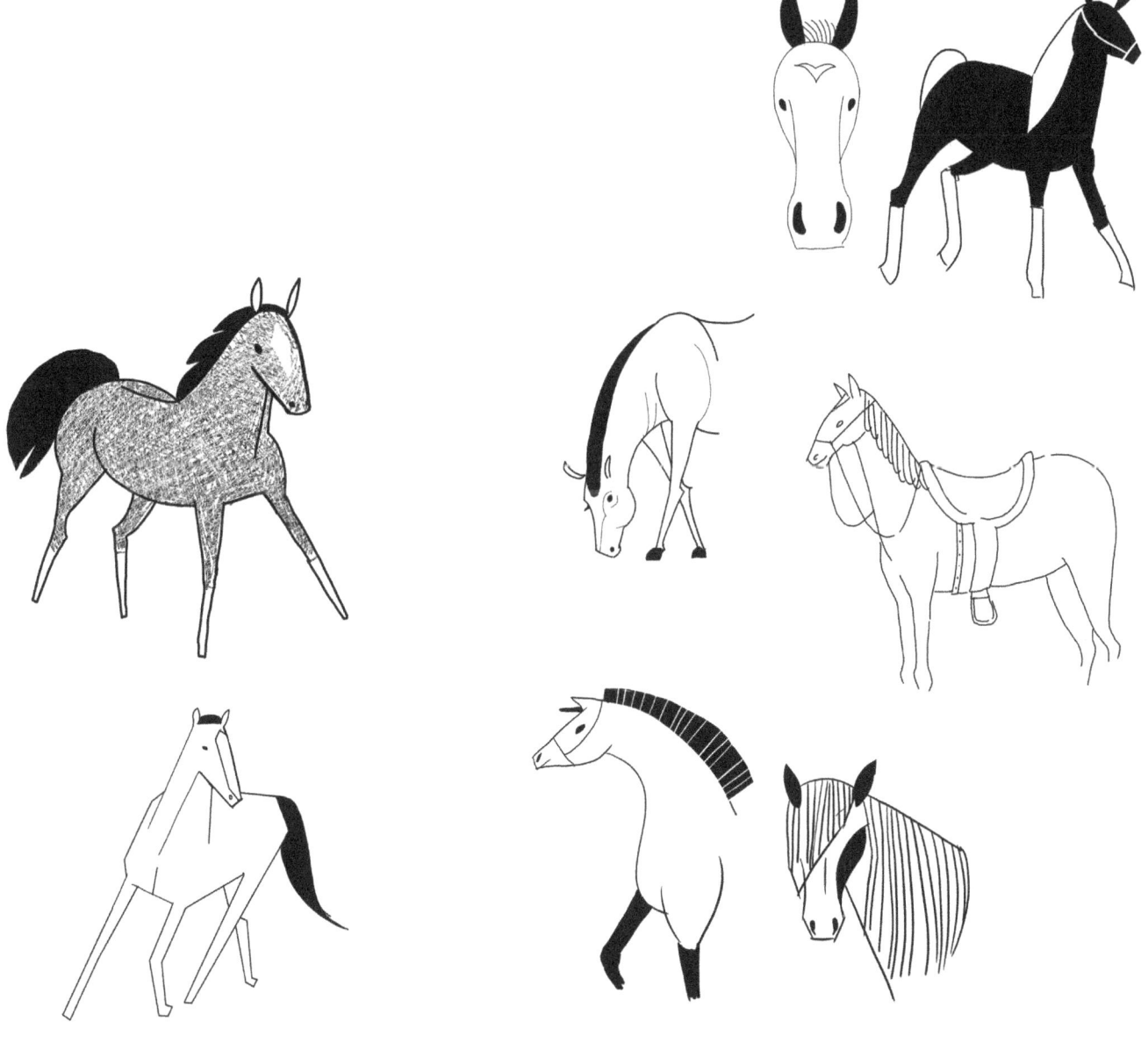

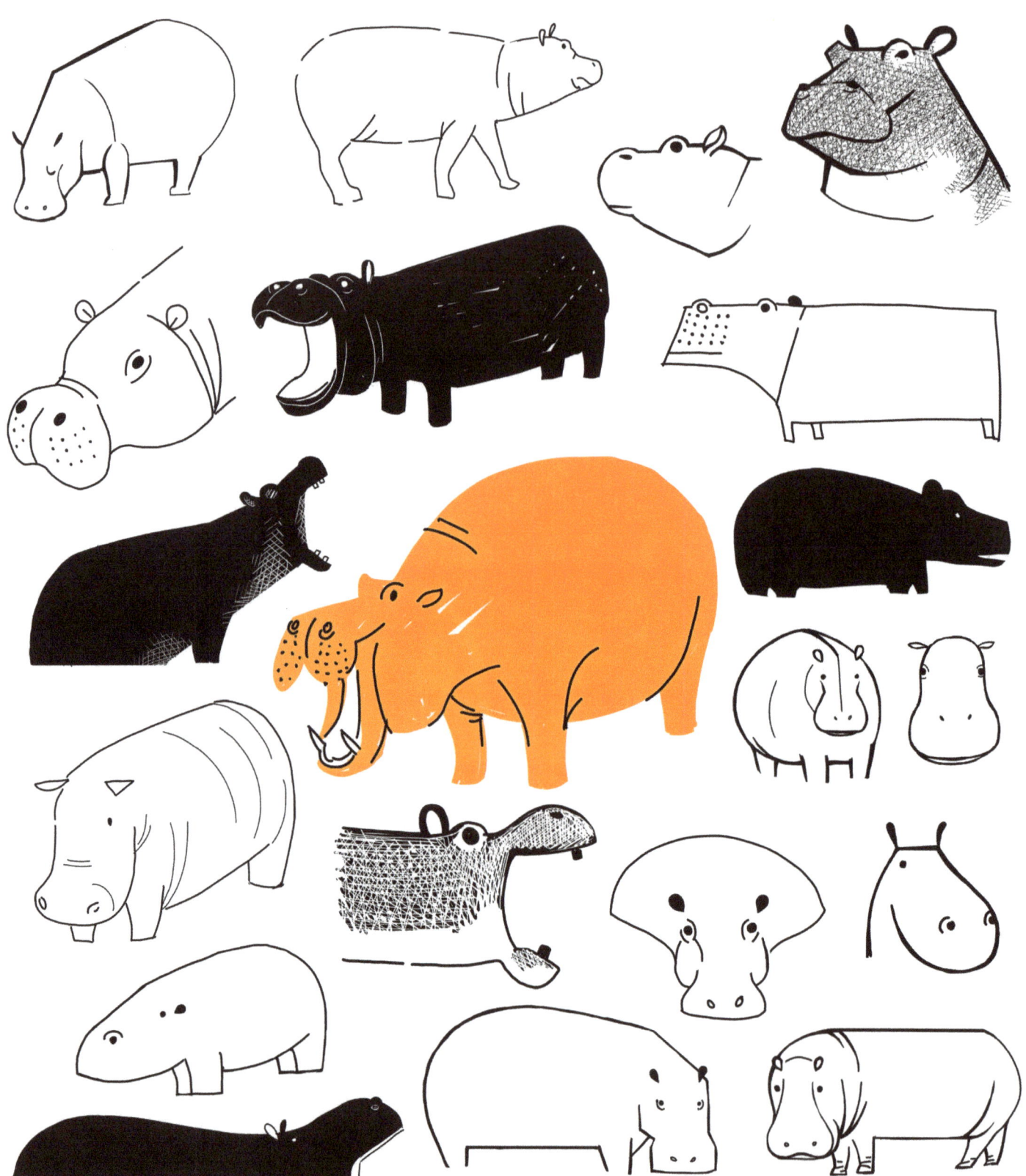

DRAW 20
hippopotamuses

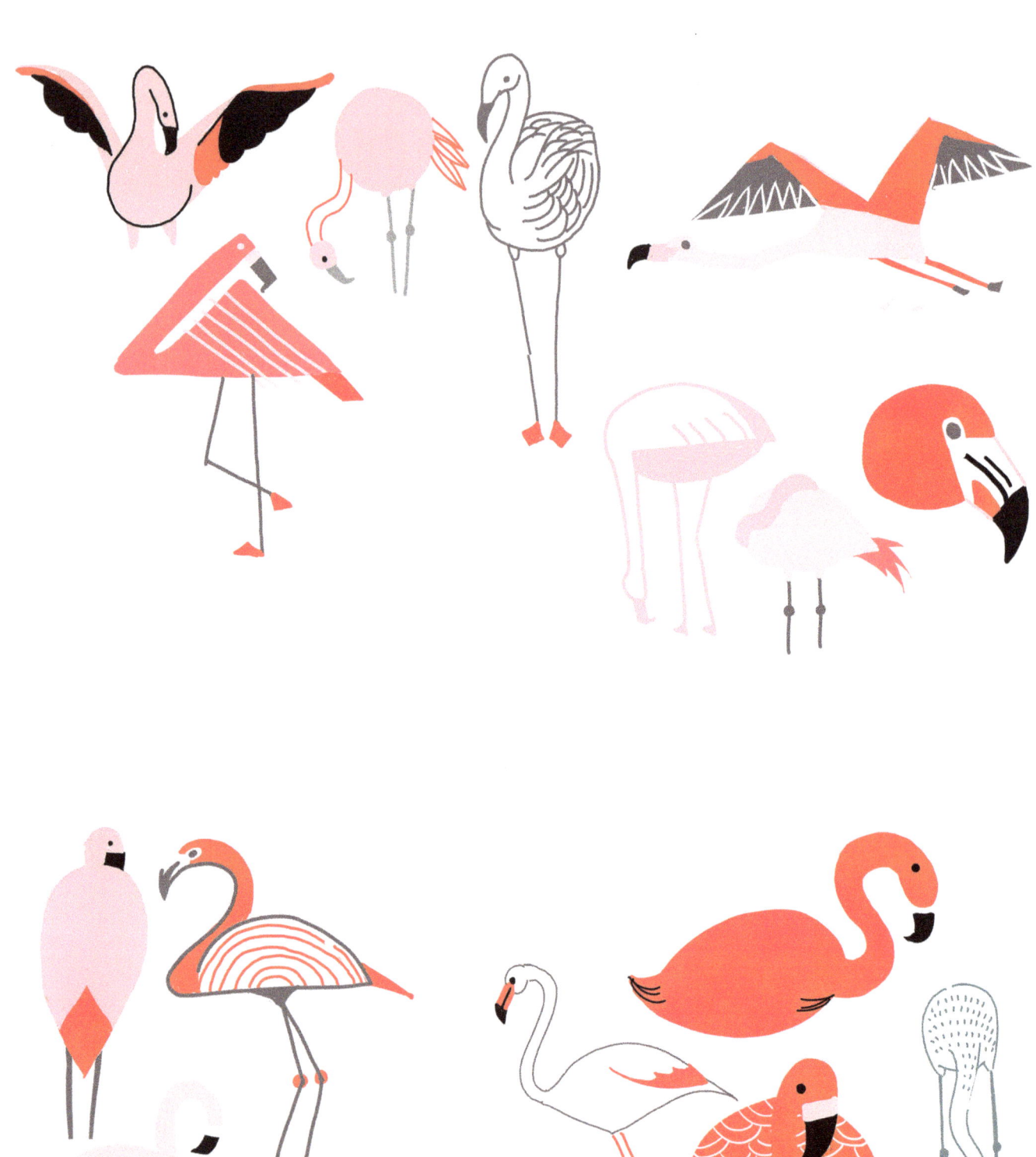

DRAW 20
FLAMINGOS

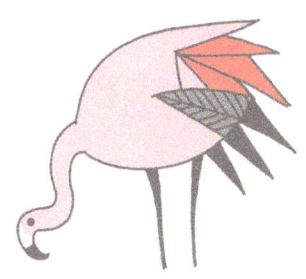

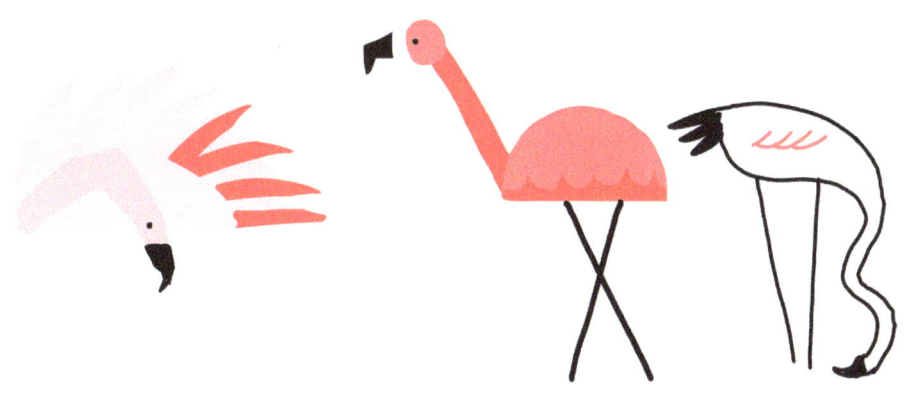

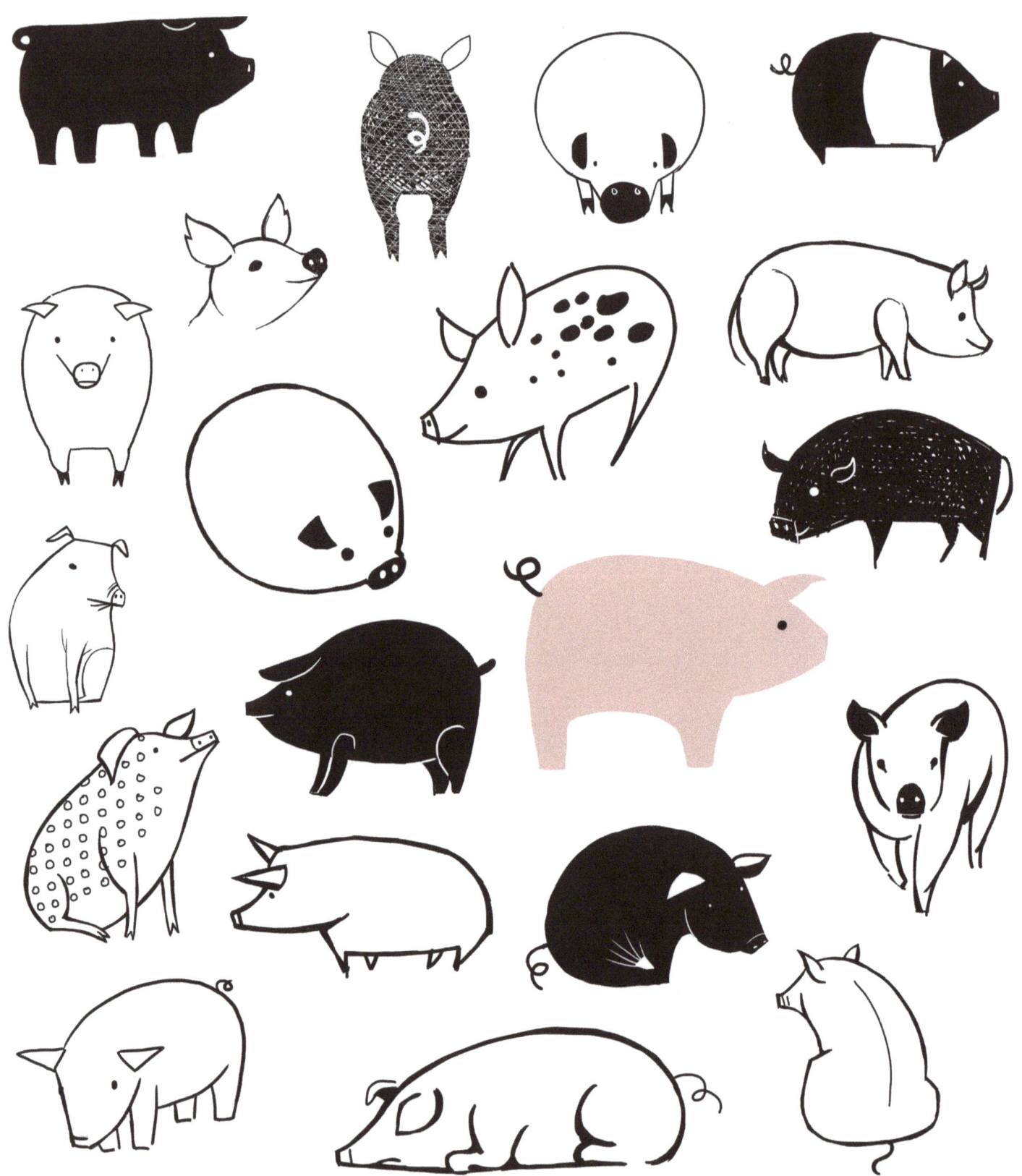

DRAW 20
PIGS

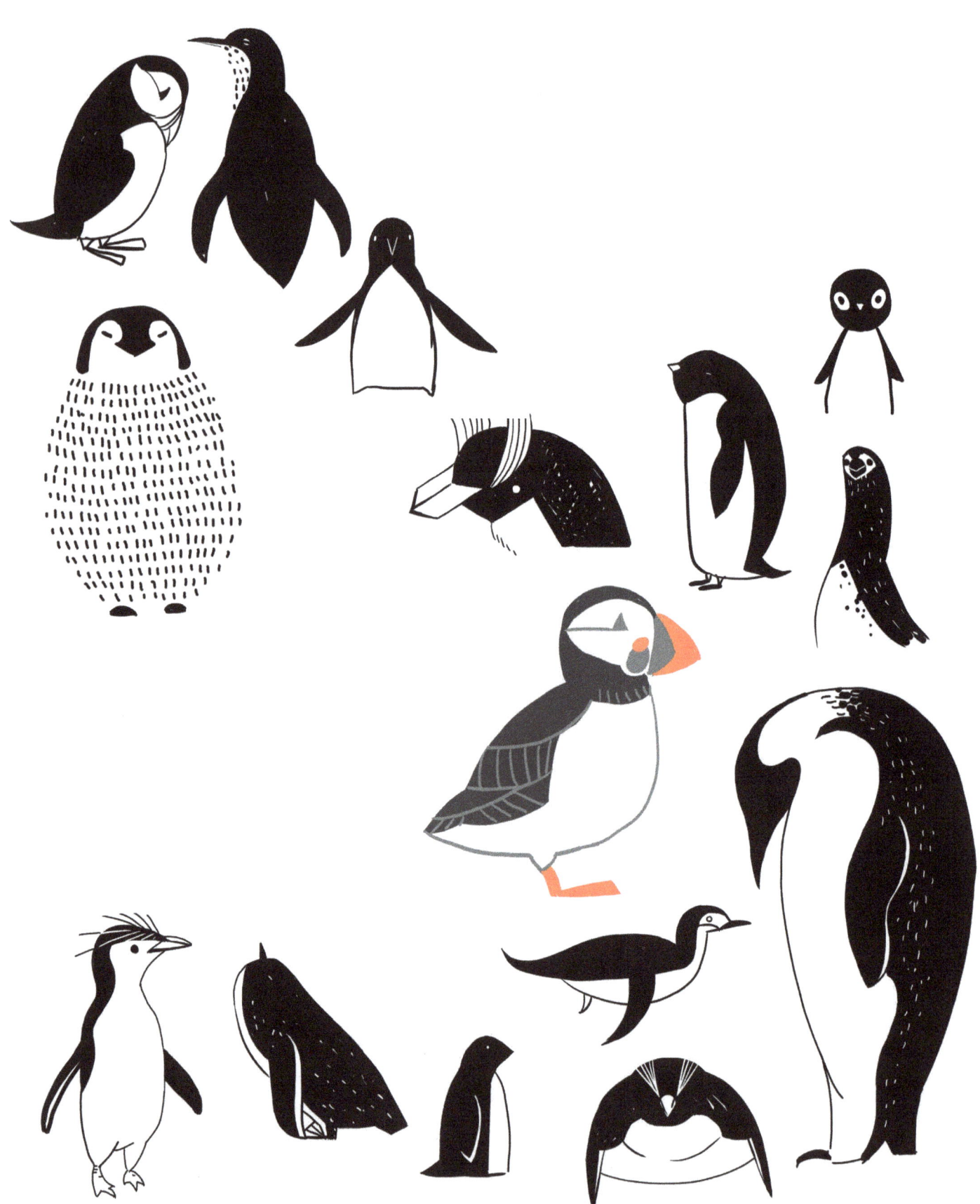

DRAW 20
penguins & puffins

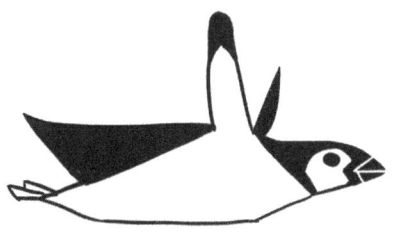

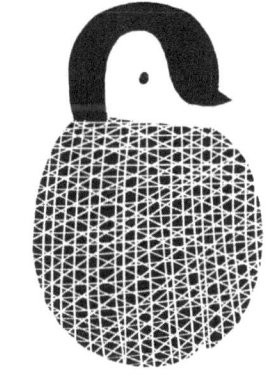

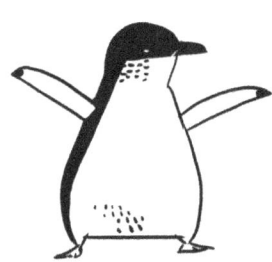

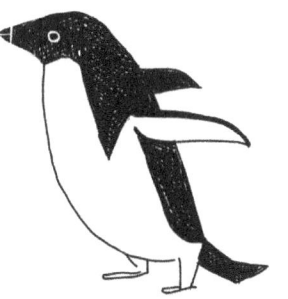

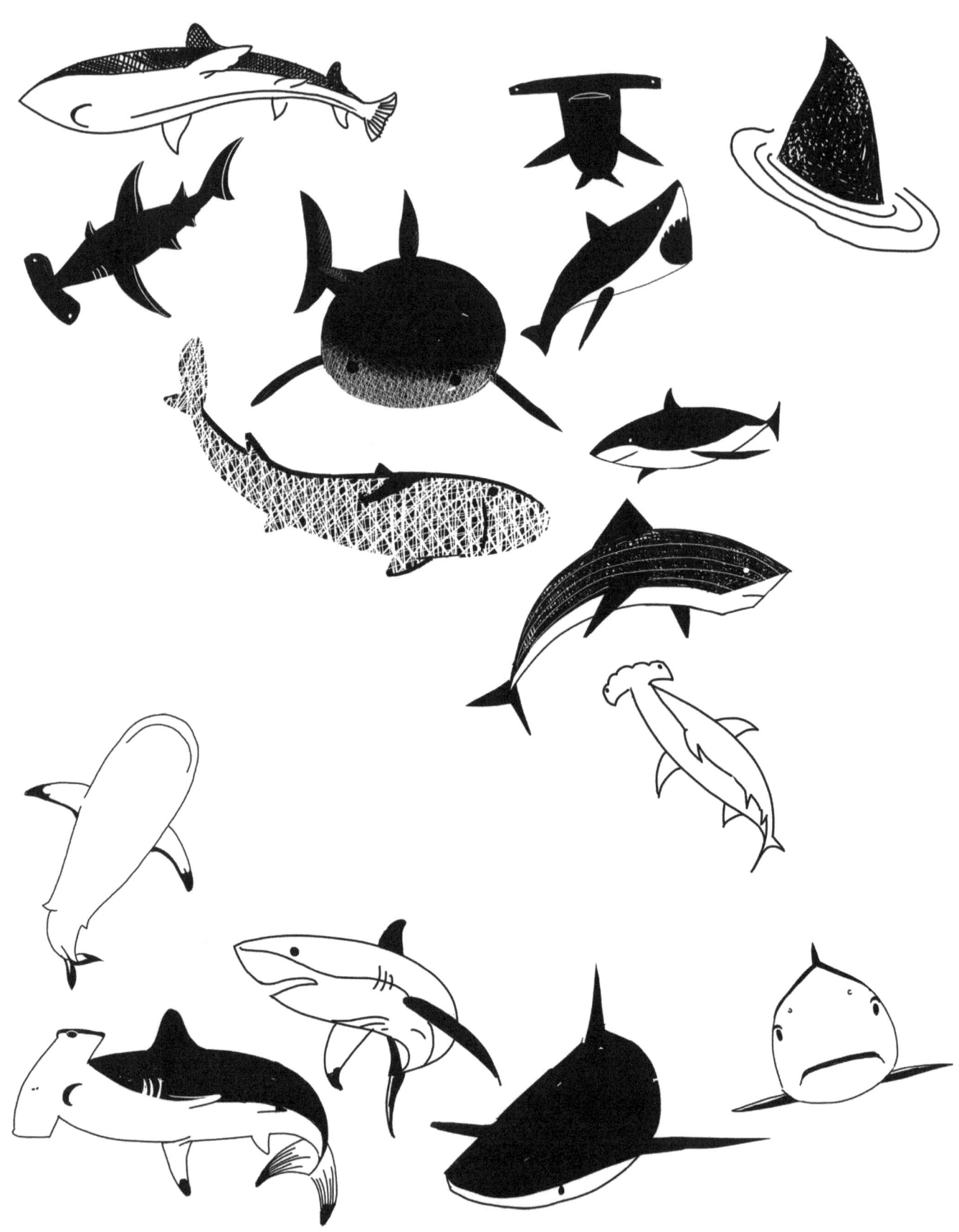

DRAW 20
SHARKS

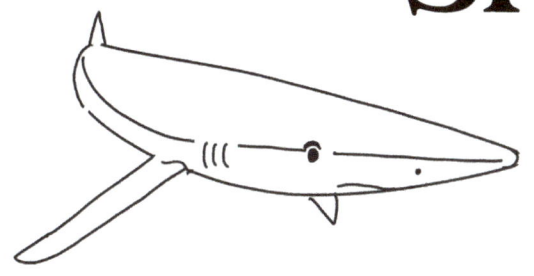
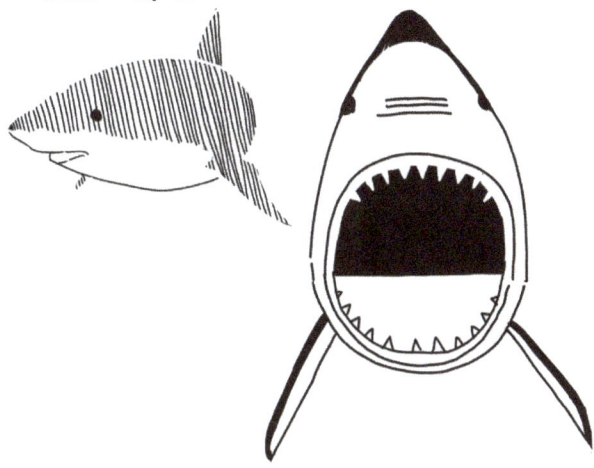
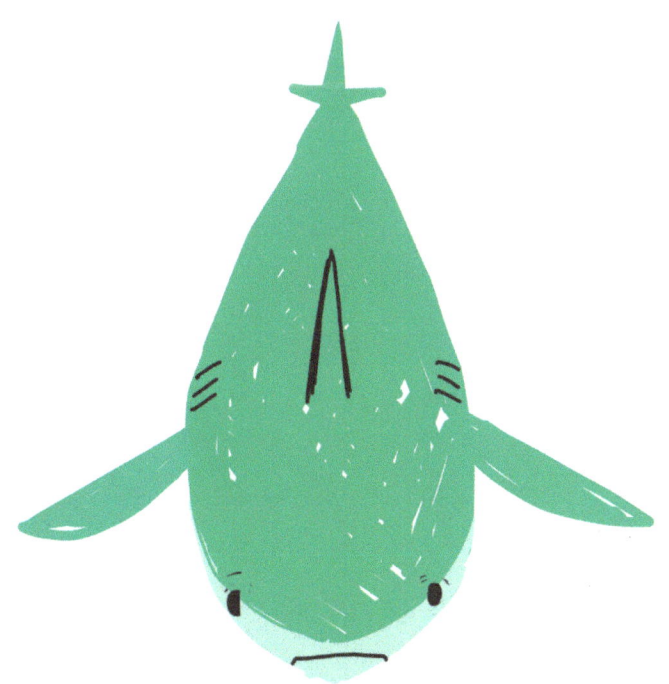
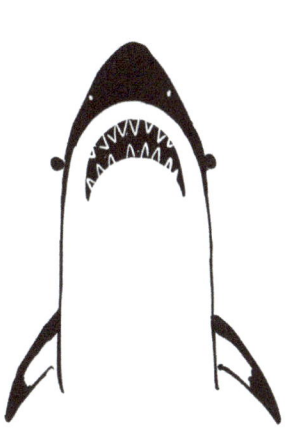

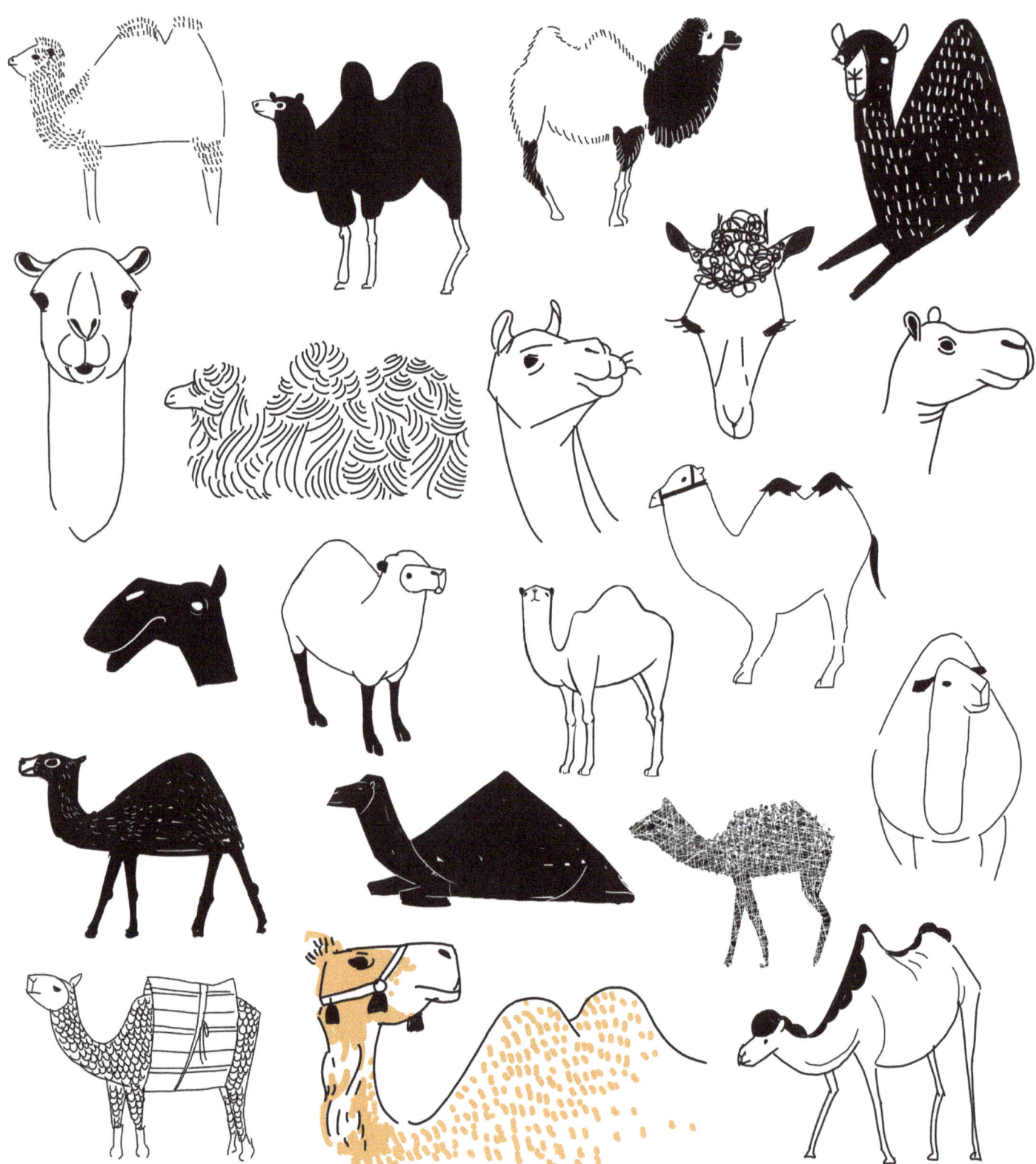

DRAW 20 camels

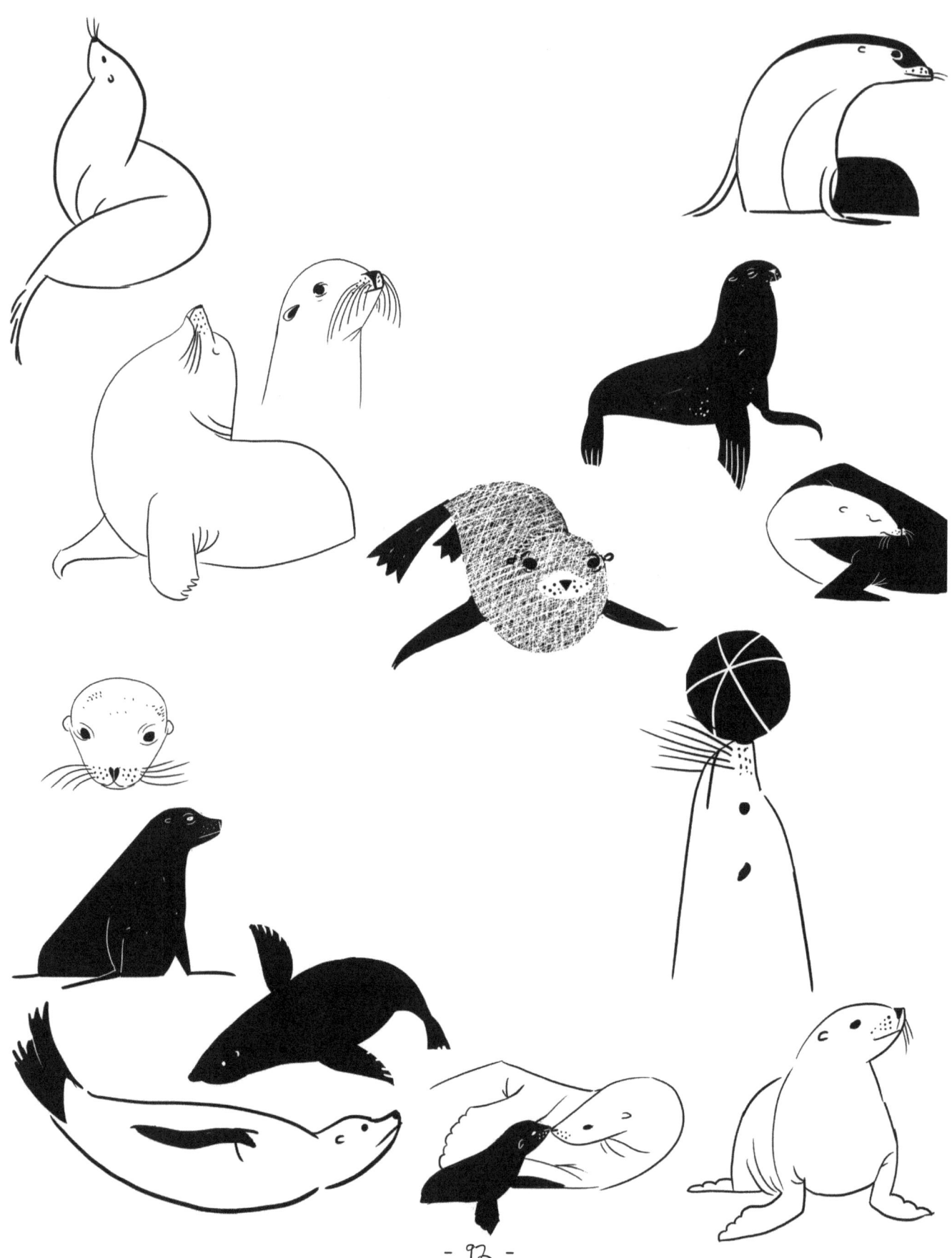

DRAW 20
sea lions

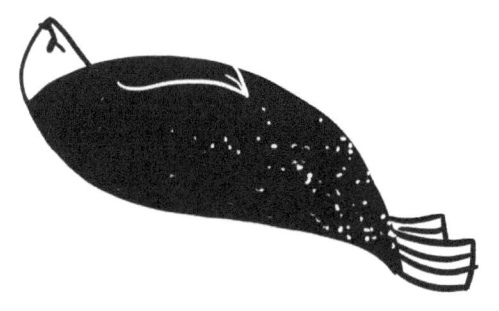
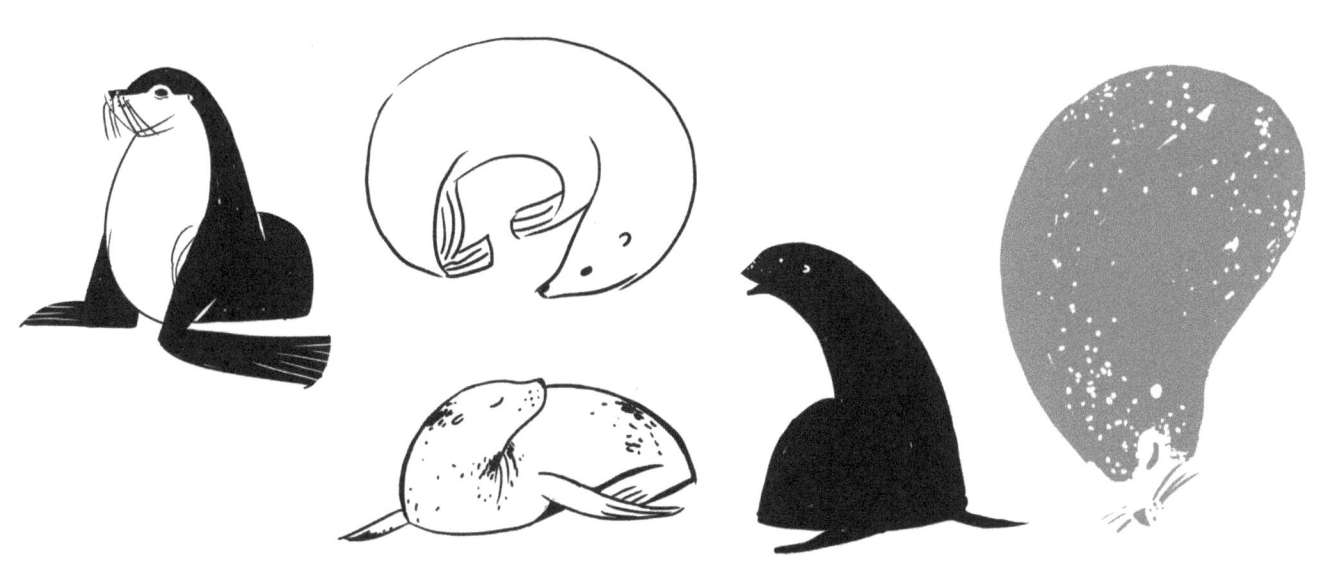

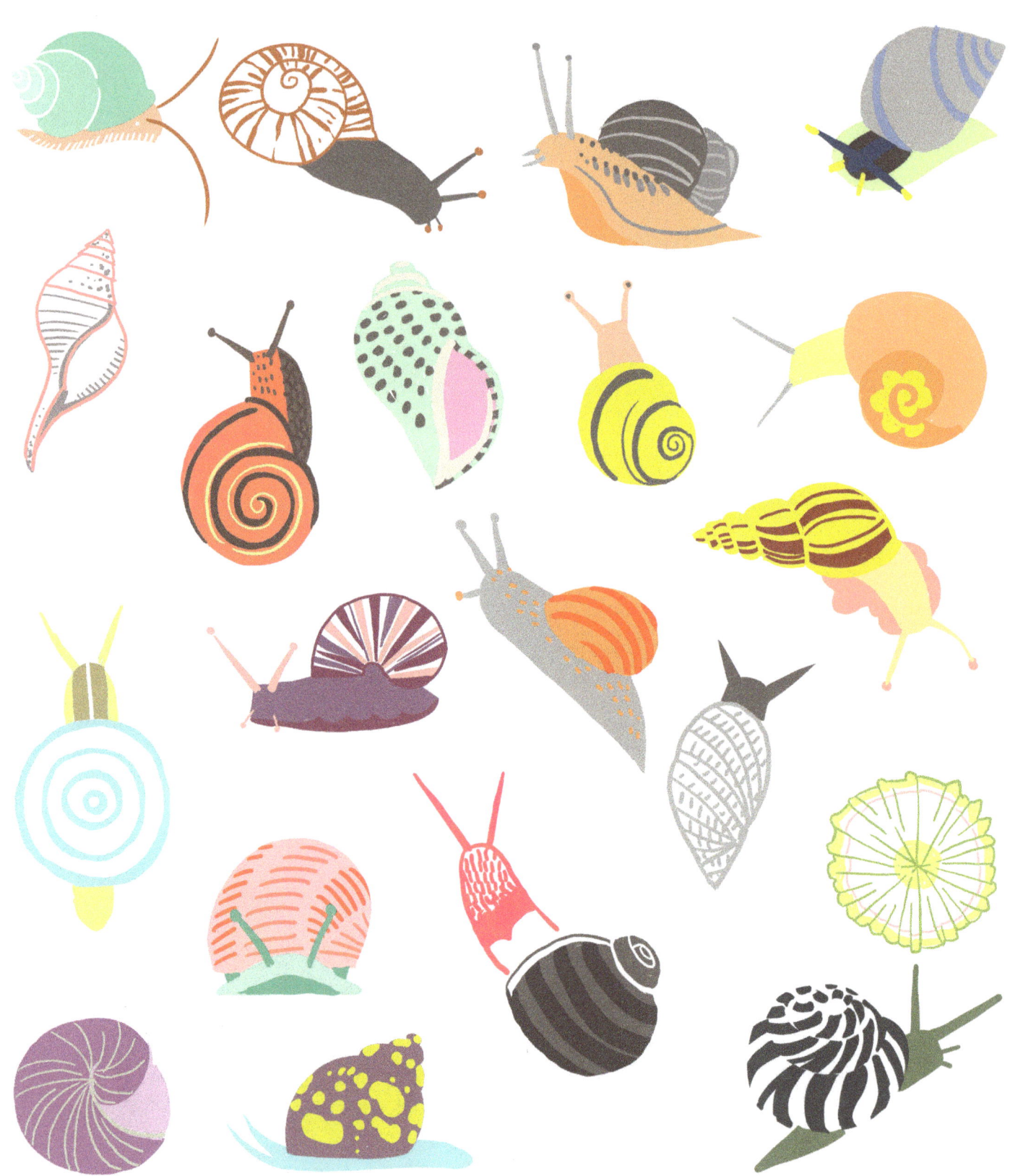

DRAW 20
snails

ABOUT THE ARTIST

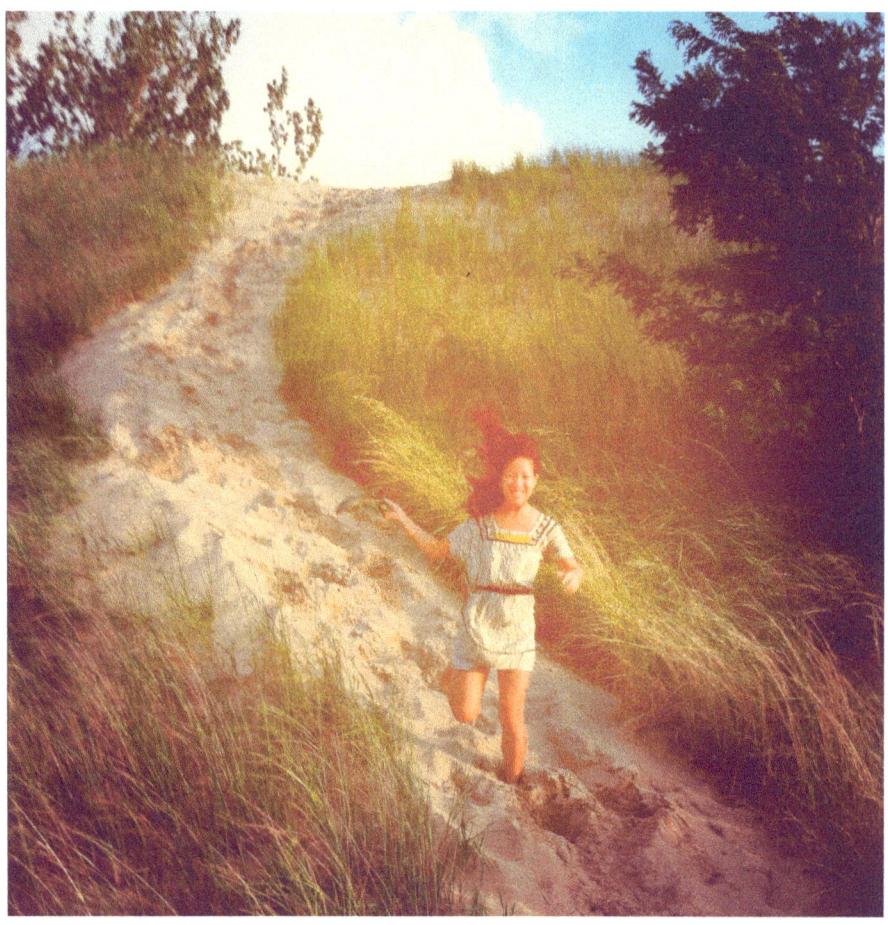

Julia Kuo grew up in Los Angeles and studied illustration and marketing at Washington University in St. Louis. She currently works as a freelance illustrator in Chicago. Julia designs stationery, illustrates children's books, concert posters, and CD covers and paints in her free time. One of her gallery shows featured paintings of street fashion shots from Face Hunter. Julia's clients include American Greetings, the *New York Times*, Little, Brown and Company, Simon and Schuster, Capitol Records, and Universal Music Group. She is also part of The Nimbus Factory, a collective of two designers and two illustrators specializing in paper goods. Her illustrations have been honored in *American Illustration, CMYK* magazine, and *Creative Quarterly*. juliakuo.com

www.ingramcontent.com/pod-product-compliance
Lightning Source LLC
Chambersburg PA
CBHW041924180526
45172CB00014B/1377